Self-Esteem and Early Learning

Key People from Birth to School

Series listing
Marian Whitehead: *Developing Language and Literacy with Young Children*
2nd edition 2002
Rosemary Roberts: *Self-Esteem and Early Learning* 3rd edition 2006
Cath Arnold: *Child Development and Learning 2–5 Years – Georgia's Story* 1999
Pat Gura: *Resources for Early Learning – Children, Adults and Stuff* 1996
Chris Pascal and Tony Bertram: *Effective Early Learning – Case Studies in Improvement* 1997
Mollie Davies: *Helping Children to Learn through a Movement Perspective* 1995

All titles are available from Paul Chapman Publishing
http://www.paulchapmanpublishing.co.uk

The 0–8 series
The 0–8 series, edited by Professor Tina Bruce, deals with essential themes in early childhood which concern practitioners, parents and children. In a practical and accessible way, the series sets out a holistic approach to work with young children, families and their communities. It is evidence based, drawing on theory and research. The books are designed for use by early years practitioners, and those on professional development courses, and initial teacher education courses covering the age-range 0–8.

Self-Esteem and Early Learning

Key People from Birth to School

Third edition

Rosemary Roberts

⑤SAGE

Los Angeles | London | New Delhi
Singapore | Washington DC

Sage Publications Ltd
1 Oliver's Yard
55 City Road
London EC1Y 1SP

SAGE Publications Inc
2455 Teller Road
Thousand Oaks, California 91320

SAGE Publications India Pvt Ltd
B 1/l 1 Mohan Cooperative Industrial Area
Mathura Road
New Delhi 110 044

SAGE Publications Asia-Pacific Pte Ltd
33 Pekin Street 02-01
Far East Square
Singapore 048763

British Library Cataloguing in Publication Data

ISBN-10 1-4129-2280-1   ISBN-13 978-1-4129-2280-7
ISBN-10 1-4129-2281-X   ISBN-13 978-1-4129-2281-4 (pbk)

Library of Congress Control Number: 2006927956

Typeset by Dorwyn, Wells, Somerset
Printed and bound by Ashford Colour Press Ltd, Gosport, Hampshire
Printed on paper from sustainable resources

For my expanding family, with love

Contents

Preface

Rosemary Roberts is an experienced practitioner, well known among policy makers in the early years field. She has been honoured with an OBE for her work. In the updated third edition of this book, she has added to the 'self-esteem and early learning' of the title, 'key people from birth to school'; thus acknowledging the perspectives of children and adults together throughout the book which form the basis of the key person approach.

Rosemary has framed the book as a story about a family situation, weaving into the story the issues that families will meet. The story shows how each family is different, but also that each family shares with others some aspects of living with young children. The reader meets a variety of situations with the family, and explores these through the character of the teenage girl who lives with them. The author stresses the importance of children being unconditionally accepted, and being allowed to have bad feelings as well as good. She shows how adults can give children the support they need, while setting limits in ways which help children to develop and learn in their widening social network.

This third edition, with its chronological narrative and accompanying commentary, offers the reader those very perspectives and understandings that facilitate warm, appropriate key person relationships both at home and in day-care. It will be a particularly useful resource for all those training to work with babies and young children from birth to school.

Tina Bruce, series editor
June 2006

Acknowledgements

First, I want to thank the two families who welcomed me into their homes week after week for two years; especially 'Lily' and 'Joe' and their mothers. For all the insights and pleasure they gave me, I owe them more than I can say.

I am particularly grateful to Chris Athey, Daphne Briggs and John Howson for all their comments and help, so willingly given; and also for this third edition to Pamela May.

Above all, my thanks are due to Tina Bruce, whose suggestion it was that I should write this book. Her consistent encouragement, confidence and assistance enabled me to complete it.

Thank you to all the children, families and colleagues with whom I have worked and from whom I have learned so much: in various places, particularly at Elms Road and at PEEP.

Finally a special thank you to my own family and friends; for their interest and support and for all that they have taught me.

Preface for the 0–8 series

The 0–8 series has stood the test of time, maintaining a central place among early childhood texts. Practitioners have appreciated the books because, while very practical, the series presents a holistic approach to work with young children, which values close partnership with families and their communities. It is evidence based, drawing on theory and research in an accessible way.

The 0–8 series continues to deal with the themes of early childhood which have always been of concern and interest to parents, practitioners and the children themselves. Each author has made an important contribution in their field of expertise, using this within a sound background of child development and practical experience with children, families, communities, schools and other early childhood settings. The Series consistently gives a central place to the interests and needs of children, emphasising the relationship between child development and the socio-cultural learning with which biological and brain development is inextricably linked.

The basic processes of communication, movement, play, self-esteem and understanding of self and others, as well as the symbolic layerings in development (leading to dances, reading, writing, mathematical and musical notations, drawing, model-making) never cease to fascinate those who love and spend time with children. Some of the books in this series focus on these processes of development and learning, by looking at children and their contexts in a general way, giving examples as they go. Other books take a look at particular aspects of individual children and the community. Some emphasise the importance of rich physical and cultural provision and careful consideration of the environment indoors and outdoors and the way that adults work with children.

I look forward to seeing the impact of the 0–8 series on the next decade.

Professor Tina Bruce
Roehampton University
June 2006

Introduction

Parents, and other people who live and work with children, often say they mind about three things. First, that children are happy; second, that they are learning successfully; and third, that they are growing up into caring and responsible adults. This book is about these three things: children's feelings, their learning, and their place in society. It offers the reader a picture of attachment as the basis of mental health.

Running like a thread from chapter to chapter is the subject of children's self-concept and the development of their self-esteem. This is seen in this book to be at the heart of how children feel, how they learn and how they relate to other people.

Although the surroundings in which most children grow up have changed greatly in the course of the last century, diversity and bi-lingualism are increasingly the norm, and ideas of what to do with babies and children keep on changing too, nonetheless the range of young children's feelings remains the same. We cannot remember many of our own feelings in early childhood; but for all of us, our parents and our children, the emotional map was, and still is, the same. This is why it is appropriate to retain many references from the last century – those thinkers and writers much of whose work forms the foundations of our current thinking.

This book proposes the importance of some of the features of that emotional map in relation to our changing world and what we now know about how children learn. The book is written for the important people – parents, teachers, staff in early childhood care and education settings and integrated Children's Centres – who have, or will have, responsibility for children and who therefore, like it or not, have power and influence over them.

The book's purpose is to use the realisation that 'we've all been there' to manage more successfully and happily the challenge of living with children and their feelings, at home or at work. It suggests that we look for a sense of balance in a range of complicated situations: for instance, understanding the child's point of view as well as our own; accepting the normality of bad feelings as well as good ones; finding ways of accepting feelings at the same time as setting limits for behaviour. Often we need to remember the other side of the coin, rather than being 'admirably single-minded'. Perhaps, as we strive for integration in early childhood, we need a new virtue for our time: multi-mindedness.

How this book is organised

The book falls into six parts, covering the period from birth to school. The first chapter in each part is mainly about the *child's* point of view. The second chapter in each part focuses more on what it feels like to be the *adult* and on ways in which adults can make the most of opportunities to support the children with whom we live and work. The chapters consist of story episodes, key statements, and explanatory text. At the end of each part there are questions to think about, and also recommended reading – 'good reads' both for adults and for sharing with babies and young children. Readers may also find browsing the index a helpful way of locating subject matter.

About the story sections

The chapters consist of story and comment. The story sections, always in italics, are based on the author's observations of children and their families from various cultural backgrounds, at home and at school; although none of the characters directly represents any particular individual.

   The story is told by Joanne, whose identity is explained in the Prologue (on the next page). Joanne is a young girl living with the family of the story, who narrates a series of reflective observations throughout the book and ends by deciding to go to College to study young children.

About the key statements and postscripts

Each of the six parts contains three key statements. In the first chapter of each part these are considered from the child's point of view, and in the second from an adult perspective. These key statements are collected together in the Postscript at the end of each part, together with questions intended to generate further thinking and discussion.

About the 'good reads'

There are also suggestions for further reading: one 'good read' per section for practitioners, and two very special picture books for sharing with babies and young children. These picture books are intended for one-to-one sharing, where adult and child can cuddle up and share the jokes, the stories and the pictures together.

Prologue

'My name is Joanne, I live with Mum and the kids, and their dad. Mum isn't my real mum, although I wouldn't mind if she was. The kids' dad isn't my dad either; he knew my real mum when I was a baby and she was very ill. My dad's not around now.

I came to live with them three years ago, when I was fifteen. Joe was just born then and Lily was two.'

PART 1

BABIES FIRST

1

Children learning to be lovable

– INTRODUCING JOE –

❛'What do you want?' Mum often mutters this to herself while she watches one of them with that friendly puzzled look. I like hearing her say that, I think it makes them feel safe. All the time I've been living with Mum and their dad, she's been watching them; not in an interfering way but because she loves them and wants to know about them. That's why they feel so safe. Sometimes I think she watches me a bit too. I hope so.

Once Joe and Lily (she's his sister) were sitting in the big bath upstairs having a great time playing. I love the way Joe looks in the bath. His curls go even tighter; and his skin is lovely and dark like his dad's. Mum was holding the towel and looking at his hair – it always looks like it's a bird's nest at the back these days.

'Joe, what shall we do with your hair?' He stopped playing and looked back at her.

'What shall we do?' she asked again. He filled the little pot he had in his hand with water and lifted it towards his head as if he was going to pour it over his hair.

'Oh no, don't get it all wet as well!,' Mum said hastily. Joe watched her anxiously holding the back of his head with his other hand.

'Mum?' he said, doubtfully. 'Mum?'

'We'd better wash your face,' she said. Joe screwed it up to be ready for the horrible moment, knowing it would make her laugh. When she laughs, he knows she loves him.

The kids' dad was really upset last week. I heard him telling one of his friends how awful it is when your baby doesn't want you. I know Joe does love his dad, and they play lots of games, but Joe had been really miserable. Mum and their dad sometimes call him 'Double Trouble', and that day he was. The others were fed up too; Lily said she wouldn't be so naughty. (Wouldn't she just?) Mum said she's never caught up on sleep since he was born, but he always used to be so good in the daytime that she managed the nights somehow. Mum said she can't keep feeding him all night, but that's what he wants, and now he's being furious and miserable all the time. I saw him really hurt himself the other day when he wanted another biscuit, and Mum said, 'No'. He was in such a rage that he banged his head on the washing machine by mistake and cried and cried.

Today was better; though. Mum and Joe and I were in the kitchen, and Mum was telling me about her friend who is having a new baby. I think Joe thought Mum was smiling at him, and he gave her a great big grin. When she noticed, she stopped talking and grinned back at him. The kitchen was really quiet, and Joe crawled over to where she was standing by the sink. He bent right over and rested his forehead on her feet and he looked so loving and helpless. After that, he looked up at her; and he was still grinning! So Mum picked him up and gave him a big hug. **9**

Babies and young children need to be accepted by their important people

Mothers and other important people

Who are babies' and young children's 'important people'? Of course, parents are important, and also – if there are any – are brothers and sisters; then there are other members of the family, friends, key people in day-care, teachers . . . and so the circle gradually widens. But let's start at the beginning – the very beginning. For nine months, the baby has been completely surrounded by the mother, and, although we are only beginning to find out about the baby's life in the womb, there can be no doubt that, when a baby is born, the baby and the mother have already learned things about each other through their bodies that no one else can possibly know. This makes the mother the first 'important person' (Winnicott, 1964, pp. 19–24).

The first important person usually, although by no means always, continues to be the mother (Holmes, 1993, pp. 75–7). But what about fathers? And what about other key people? Many fathers would say that their baby knew them right from the start. We cannot be sure of the reasons for this, although it is certainly often the case (Brazelton, 1992, p. 35). Whether the answer is to be found in nature or nurture or a combination of both, one thing is clear: a baby must come to know someone before he or she is able to see that person as 'important'. In attachment theory, as the mother is the first important person, she acts as the mediator for the baby's subsequent important people, who are, initially, substitutes for her, and who may sooner or later come to be just as important. This attachment often happens with fathers who share much of the childcare and take over the role of the mother in many ways.

Early brain development: some tentative messages

Awareness of the importance of development in the earliest years of life has risen dramatically over the period 1975–2005, especially in relation to brain development. Various factors have fed this awareness of the importance of the earliest years. In her Fulbright Lecture (2000) entitled 'The Brain Debate', Dr Anne Meade wrote:

There is a convergence of findings from neuroscience, cognitive science, development psychology and early childhood education research. Generally, there is agreement that enriched environments such as are found in high quality early childhood settings facilitate the adaptive changes to children's brains. The enrichment of social relationships – of adult–child interactions – is especially important, remembering of course that the brain is malleable and the changes in response to relationship experience can be both positive and negative for the child.

Meade suggested that brain research does validate and explain many observational/clinical findings, and that imaging research is showing where, when and what is unusual in brain functioning in people with learning and behavioural disorders. While emphasising that behavioural neuroscience is still in its infancy, she draws some tentative conclusions from research about appropriate early experiences for brain development which include the following:

- The quality of interpersonal relationships, i.e. adult–child interactions, is very important. An adult tuning into and responding to the child's mental state allows his or her brain to develop a capacity to balance emotions and thinking skills.
- Experiences for young children need to address their need for stimulation of all the senses and the associated brain regions. Multi-modal activity – involving the senses, motor skills and thinking – is important.
- Play addresses the brain's need for multi-sensory, multi-modal experiences. Animal studies suggest that the play needs to include social, complex and challenging experiences.
- Provision for the development of implicit memories is likely to be more fruitful than direct instruction, as the brain circuits for explicit memories do not mature until the age of 3 or 4 years. Implicit memories are built by diverse exposures to an array of inputs in naturalistic settings.

The authors of *How Babies Think* (Gopnik *et al.*, 1999), in a compelling opening paragraph, describe a newborn baby through the lens of our new perspective:

Walk upstairs, open the door gently, and look in the crib. What do you see? Most of us see a picture of innocence and helplessness, a clean slate. But, in fact, what we see in the crib is the greatest mind that has ever existed, the most powerful learning machine in the universe. The tiny fingers and mouth are exploration devices that probe the alien world around them with more precision than any Mars rover. The crumpled ears take a buzz of incomprehensible noise and flawlessly turn it into meaningful language. The wide eyes that sometimes seem to peer into your very soul actually do just that, deciphering your deepest feelings. The downy head surrounds a brain that is forming millions of new connections every day. That, at least, is what thirty years of scientific research have told us. (p. 1)

Certainly our perception of how children develop has shifted in important ways. Shore (1997, p. 18) offers a fascinating glimpse into how our understanding of young children's development has changed.

OLD THINKING	NEW THINKING
How a brain develops depends on the **genes** you are born with	How a brain develops depends on the complex **interplay** between the **genes** you are born with and the **experiences** you have
The **experiences** you have before age three have a **limited impact** on later development	Early **experiences** have a **decisive impact** on the architecture of the brain, and on the nature and extent of adult capacities
A **secure relationship** with a primary caregiver creates a favourable **context** for early development and learning	**Early interactions** don't just create a context; they **directly affect** the way the **brain is 'wired'**
Brain development is **linear**: the brain's capacity to learn and change grows steadily as an infant progresses towards childhood	Brain development is **non-linear**: there are prime times for developing different kinds of knowledge and skills
A toddler's brain is much **less active** than the brain of a college student.	By the time children reach age three, their brains are **twice as active** as those of adults. Activity drops during adolescence.

What does all this mean for child development, and is there a straightforward message for parents and practitioners? One researcher says that there is such a message, for parents, practitioners and for government policy:

> *The bottom line message from research on the early years is that quality matters. This leads to a clear policy conclusion: policies should aim to support parents in providing good-quality care themselves, and in arranging good-quality child care.* (Waldfogel, 2004, p. 25)

And drawing on a range of studies and reviews (Blau, 2001; Shonkoff and Phillips, 2000; Smolensky and Gootman, 2003; Vandell and Wolfe, 2000) Waldfogel says:

> *For young children, what defines quality is that the care they receive – whether from a parent or a non-parental caregiver – is sensitive and responsive to their individual needs.* (p. 6)

These findings – focusing on the importance of close relationships in the earliest years – are clearly reflected in very many excellent summaries of recent brain research, together with strong acknowledgements of their implications for parents and practitioners. The first four principles underpinning the UK's 'Birth to Three Matters' framework (Sure Start, 2002, p. 3) also emphasised the importance of young children's relationships:

- *Parents and families are central to the well-being of the child.*
- *Relationships with other people (both adults and children) are of crucial importance in a child's life.*
- *A relationship with a key person at home and in the setting is essential to young children's well-being.*
- *Babies and young children are social beings, they are competent learners from birth.*

Focusing further, it is the third principle, 'A relationship with a key person at home and in the setting is essential to young children's well-being', which has particular practical relevance for parents and carers of the youngest children – those key people who make such a difference.

In *The Learning Brain: Lessons for Education* (2005) Sarah-Jayne Blakemore and Uta Frith look at what is known now about the developing brain, and examine implications for the wider sweep of education policy and practice. This book takes in a range of issues (for instance the resilience of the brain beyond the age of three, numeracy and literacy, the brain in adolescence, learning and remembering) that are relevant both to primary and to secondary schools. In contrast to the view that birth to three is the most influential period of the developing brain, this book emphasises the brain's plasticity; and in relation both to the environment in the first three years and to nutrition, the authors point out that 'in both cases . . . too little is damaging, but we know very little about the effects of too much' (p. 186). In summary they argue that 'learning is not limited to childhood . . . learning can be lifelong'.

However, a robust review of the research and its implications from the US (Shonkoff and Philips, 2000) has been enormously influential in its conclusion that 'what happens during the first months and years of life matters a lot . . . early pathways, though far from indelible, establish either a sturdy or fragile stage on which subsequent development is constructed'. (p. 384)

Nurturing relationships is clearly the stuff of home life in a baby's first year (see the anecdote about Joe and his mum in 'Introducing Joe'); but what if Mum is at work and Joe is in day-care? This question has generated much of the emphasis that is now placed on the importance of the 'key person approach' in day-care, described by Elfer *et al.* (2003, p. 19) in *Key Persons in the Nursery* as 'an emotional relationship as well as an organisational strategy'. Edwards (2002) in *Relationships and Learning* offers a framework to support caring for children which also focuses on relationships.

Finally Sue Gerhardt, writing incisively about the implications of the research on early brain development, emphasises the importance of parents. Here she flags up the need for a sea change:

To provide more children with the optimal start for being emotionally equipped to deal with life, we need to invest in early parenting. This investment will be costly. To bring about conditions where every baby has the kind of responsive care that he or she needs to develop well means that the adults who do this work must be valued and supported in their task. This in itself would involve a sea change in our cultural attitudes. (Gerhardt, 2004, p. 217)

Now that we know more about children's brain development from birth to school, we still need to ask what it means. What are the implications for parents and practitioners, the 'essential key people' referred to earlier? What do we need to think about? This question is explored mainly chronologically (from birth to school) in a variety of ways, in the six sections of this book.

Earliest learning

Babies can already do many important things when they are born. They can breathe, digest, protest, respond, interact and, most important of all, they can learn (Gopnik *et al.*, 1999). They are, however, completely dependent on others for food, warmth and love and they learn naturally in order to survive. In the womb, the rate of learning has been gradual, and the experiences relatively controlled; then, from the moment of birth, the rate of learning suddenly accelerates. Perhaps this accelerated learning is like a hectic toboggan ride. Starting steadily along the brow of the hill, the baby is suddenly pushed onto the steep slope and hurtles down, unable to stop or go back. Gradually adjusting to the breathtaking speed, the baby begins to make some sense of the surroundings as they flash by and starts to realise the possibilities of steering the toboggan.

In that first headlong plunge of the first year, the baby needs to feel safe, with some sense of being held and the knowledge that someone is there to steer for the time being. Within the womb, there was never, of course, any question about someone being there; but at birth, just when the landscape changes dramatically and the baby needs 'holding' most urgently, the mother becomes much less reliable. In fact, now that she is not attached, she sometimes even goes away. The baby needs food, warmth and love, and reassurance that he or she will not be abandoned (Purves and Selleck, 1999).

Unconditional acceptance

Before birth, a baby is 'contained' – physically – by the mother; it is this containment that keeps the baby safe, so that he or she can grow. After birth, although that containment can never again be so absolute, the baby's mother and other important people continue to provide substitutes for it. It is reflected in the mother's physical care and also in the way in which she 'holds' the baby in her mind, accepting the baby's developing personality without judgement. For the baby, the mother's physical care is also a psychological matter (Leach, 2003, pp. 142–4, and Winnicott, 1964, p. 183). Just as they are physically dependent, so babies and young children also need to have their feelings contained by their important adults until they themselves have learned how to manage them. In this way, they are doubly dependent; learning to be acceptable is important, for physical and psychological survival.

The sort of acceptance that babies and young children need from parents and other important people is acceptance that is independent of their behaviour; it is acceptance *of the child* without reservations and without judgements. Carl Rogers described it as 'unconditional positive regard' (Rogers, 1961, p. 62). This is not to say that a parent or carer must suspend all judgements about the actions of the baby or child in question; it is simply that a parent or carer's *unconditional* acceptance *of the child him or herself* is not threatened by these judgements.

Babies learn that they are acceptable by experiencing, day by day, the results of that acceptance. Every time the father smiles at the baby, every time the mother is there when needed, the baby knows more certainly that he or she is accepted. And when the mother is not there, the baby is not so sure. Some babies take this uncertainty very calmly, while some find it intolerable. Every baby is temperamentally unique, with different responses to the whole range of emotions experienced in all cultures and places.

This kind of acceptance is important for all babies and young children and the bedrock of confidence that can develop as a result is especially crucial for those children who have a growing awareness that they are different from others. This may be because of an impairment, or because they happen to be in a minority in some way.

It is inevitable that sometimes a baby or young child will feel abandoned, and the sense of being acceptable and cared for will be threatened. Since being cared for is essential for a baby's continued existence, the baby learns about how to avoid losing the carer (Miller, 1979, p. 22). When an 'important person' smiles at the baby, and when that person comes at the baby's call, the sense that he or she is acceptable is confirmed. This is not simply a passive process; all the time the baby is learning by experience how to win the smiles, how to bring the person. Every experience is a learning experience.

– JOE'S JOKES –

❛ Joe made us laugh the other day. I love it that he's so fun to play with; anything we do, he does it too – well, almost anything. Lily was sitting on the sofa watching the telly and trying to balance him on her lap. Her lap's not quite big enough, and he was a bit wobbly but he was all right really. Anyway when Mum came near, he made this 'I'm not really safe' whimpering sort of noise and put on a pathetic face. When Mum saw it, she couldn't help laughing, and nor could I. When he saw us thinking he was funny he knew it was a joke and laughed as well. It's like when he sees you smiling at him, he always smiles back.

The way Joe thinks he's a clown and makes us laugh makes me wonder about that time when he just wouldn't eat. He was born in September; and this was round about February or March. Mum kept saying it was time to start that mushy stuff babies have, but she didn't really want to, it was everyone else saying it really. He was quite happy just with her feeding him, too. Anyway one day she decided she'd better give it a go, so she mixed some up, and he opened his mouth, and in it went. Once was enough, though! He looked so disgusted and astonished that Mum laughed but that was one time he didn't laugh too. He screwed up his face and shut his mouth really tight, and if Mum managed to get any between his gums he spat it straight out again. One time when she took the spoon away he risked opening his mouth and babbling at her crossly. It sounded exactly like he was saying, 'What are you doing this for? I've told you I hate it, why do you go on?' Quite soon after that, he opened his mouth really wide, but that was only because he got upset about it all and started to cry.

I don't think Mum really wanted him to eat mush then, anyway – she just thought he ought to. Perhaps that's why he wasn't keen either.

Why did I start talking about that? Oh yes, it's the way he thinks. He thinks he's a clown, so he makes us laugh, and he thinks he's a baby so he drinks milk from Mum. He doesn't think he's big, like Dan across the road – at least, not yet – so he doesn't go to school and he doesn't think he's big like Lily – at least, not yet – so he doesn't eat things with a spoon. It all depends what he thinks.

I know what he does think though. He thinks he can talk. Ever since the day Joe popped out, Mum's been having conversations with him. She does it all the time. When he was only a few weeks old, I saw her having one of those chats with him that you have with babies. I remember thinking that if I'd wanted to make a film, I could have dubbed it and had him saying things so easily – the tone of voice and gestures were there, it only needed the actual words. Mum likes him to tell her things, that's why. She wants him to talk, she shows him how, she knows he will one day and he knows it too.

That was more than a year ago. He doesn't have any problems with eating now. Last week Lily had her friends to tea, and they're all gannets, Mum says, although she does like it when everything gets eaten. When she said, 'Who wants some more?' Joe waved his hand in the air and shouted, 'Me!' louder than any of the others. He ate it all too. I noticed he was watching Lily really carefully and when someone asked her a question and she nodded her head, Joe nodded his too, in exactly the same way. They love it when he copies them. He thinks he's one of them now.

How babies and young children learn to see themselves is significantly affected by their growing knowledge of how to be acceptable to us

Development of self-concept

'You're the best', children might say one day, with conviction; or, on another day, 'You're nasty', with even more conviction. None of us are immune from these judgements, and each one that comes our way is like another feature added to our internal picture of who we are. By the time we are adult, most of us have grown used to our internal picture, and have found ways of rejecting judgements that don't seem to fit, although sometimes a new one gives us a jolt.

> 'Dan's mum says you're a better mum than her,' said Lily. 'But I don't think so.'
> 'Hmm,' said Mum, looking thoughtful. 'I wonder why.'

How do we build up our internal picture of who we are? An idea that occurs consistently in the discussion is that we learn about ourselves from other people and events. Particular reference has been made to the roles of 'important' people, especially parents and teachers, in the development of children's self-concept (Dowling, 2005 and Honess and Yardley, 1987).

Observation tells us that babies and young children experience a bewildering and often overwhelming range of emotions that they cannot understand or control. The mother and other important people can play an important part in seeing and understanding the infant as a whole person at a time when the infant's powerful sensations, feelings, excitements and furies act in a fragmenting way, splitting the infant's dawning self-perception (Klein, 1975a, pp. 190–2). If people respond so that the infant comes to feel wholly recognised and accepted, then the infant can recognise and accept him or herself as a whole person.

The mother's face and body are like a mirror to the baby. In this very early mirroring process, both know that they are accepted by the other. The mother's acceptance forms the basis of the baby's self-concept, and the mother's responses are the first 'brush strokes' for the developing picture.

Body language

A mother cannot pretend this early acceptance, because her baby knows her intimately in a physical way, and a mother's body language will give her away every time. A baby knows about a mother, not only by how she looks, but by how she sounds, how her body feels, maybe even by smell and taste (Gopnik *et al.*, 1999, pp. 27–8). If, as sometimes happens, a mother's feelings for her baby are very mixed at this stage, it is not the end of the world. It helps if the mother can accept these mixed feelings in herself and not struggle against them; the baby or young child may need particular understanding and very explicit unconditional acceptance later on.

So babies learn about being acceptable with their first language: that is, not by the speech that we usually mean when we refer to language, but by body language. Babies develop this way of learning and communicating in order to survive, needing it long before they know the commonly accepted meanings of spoken words. They use body language before birth and, once this way of communicating is established, they go on using it, long after they know how to understand and use spoken language. For a while, children revert to using their original way of knowing whether they are acceptable to check what people say. At first, particularly because they tend to accept the literal meanings of what we say, they often find that spoken and body language are not consistent. This can be very confusing and upsetting for them (Donaldson, 1978 and Harris, 1989).

> *'Why doesn't Dan's mummy ever smile at me when I go over there?' asked Lily. 'She said I was always welcome to go and play with Dan, but I don't think she really wants me.'*

In adulthood, and across cultures, we vary enormously in the extent to which we retain our original language – body language – for understanding and communicating feelings. Some people continue to rely on this to a large extent, some use both sorts of language, sometimes comparing the different sets of 'evidence', and others abandon the roots of their self-knowledge and put their faith in the spoken word. In the same way that we vary in how we receive communications about ourselves, we also vary in our conscious awareness of both what we actually feel and the messages we give about our feelings (Claxton, 1997 and Rogers, 1961, pp. 338–46).

Babies need genuine acceptance – mothers and other important people cannot pretend. There is a very early balancing act in the interaction between the mother and baby: as the mother consciously and unconsciously shows the baby what she recognises and accepts, the baby learns to *be* the sort of person she will recognise and accept. If she is able to recognise and accept *all* the baby's feelings as important, then the baby will be able to recognise and accept them also. The baby's developing self-perception reflects that he or she is growing into a whole person who has a mixture of feelings. Initially, a mother may accept, and thus hold, some feelings for the baby until they are manageable. Then there will come a time when, because the baby *can* accept feelings of pain, anxiety and anger as genuine and legitimate, he or she can begin to learn to deal with them.

We often talk, though, of babies as being good, lovable, awful, or difficult. All the time, and unavoidably, we give babies and young children signals about what we love in them, what we approve of and how we want them to be. It is a natural way of showing them how to be acceptable, both to us and to the world in general. The child's developing self-perception is inextricably linked with learning to be acceptable; but being acceptable sometimes means not showing pain, fear or anger. So it happens that some children learn to exclude pain, fear and anger from their perceptions of themselves: unable either to control those feelings or have them safely accepted by someone else, they manage to 'lose' them in order to be acceptable (Winnicott, 1986, pp. 65–70).

We know about losing things from the work of Piaget (1953, p. 211). Just because you can't see something, that doesn't mean it has ceased to exist (see Chapter 2).

– INTRODUCING LILY –

❛*Mum's done the same trick with Lily as with Joe. Lily thinks she can read. I was watching her the other day sitting on the floor with her back against the sofa. The floor was covered with bits of jigsaw, heaps of books, her dolls, Joe's Duplo and lots of those old conkers and fir cones from last autumn, all mixed up together. Joe was off with Mum in the kitchen, hoping for another biscuit. Lily had the Nursery Rhymes book on her lap and she was kind of leafing through it like Mum does when she's looking for a good one to sing. Sometimes Lily sang one all the way through and she nearly always got it right. She put her finger on the words, too – not the right ones, though!*

When she came to the end, she dropped it on the floor and picked the next one up off the pile, which was the one with the holes in it, about different animals. Not the caterpillar one – the one with a goat and a monkey. You're supposed to look through the holes as though the book was a mask and pretend to be that animal. When she did it, she got that far-away look, when you know she's thinking about something else completely. When she got to the lion, she started making fierce roaring noises, and thought she was going to tear us all to bits. Good thing it was a baby rabbit on the next page!

It reminded me of when she came home from playgroup pretending to be the grown-up. It was so clever of her; pretending to be someone else. She was really fed up with Joe because Mum's still feeding him. I reckon she thinks he's had Mum quite long enough, especially now Joe does more things like her – if she hasn't got Mum any more like that, why should Joe have her? Anyway she pretended to be the grown-up so that she could make Joe have the dummy that Dan's baby left behind. She knew that, as Lily she couldn't make Joe take the dummy. But as a grown-up – well, grown-ups can make anyone do anything, can't they? When Mum asked her to only pretend with the dummy and not do it for real, Lily just hit Joe. I suppose she couldn't think of another way to put him in his place – where she wants him, instead of where he is.

A couple of weeks ago, Mum had to go away for a few days. The kids' dad looked after them, and they had a great time. Lily's really funny now, though – she keeps act- ing like she's Mum. The first time she did it was when she came down and found me just taking my coat off. She put on this deep voice she uses to be grown-up and asked me if I would prefer tea or coffee! It made me feel really special, to think that she thought of asking all by herself. Then she took Joe outside into the garden and let him play with her dolls. She said they were off to visit the jungle, and when I asked what the jungle would be like, she put on the deep voice and said, 'It's got toys and dinosaurs in it'. Then she gave me a secret, laughing sort of look and added, 'and fly- ing beds in the sky.'

The next day Mum came back, and Dan's mum came over with Dan and their baby.

Dan's baby is too small to play with Joe, but Dan and Lily play a lot. Mum had to go out, so Dan's mum was keeping an eye on things – at least, that's how she saw it. Now that Lily knows how to be 'Mum', though, she thinks she can be in charge. She did help Dan's mum, but I think she thought Dan's mum was helping her. Dan needed a blanket for his game, and Lily explained that they only had duvets now, but she said he could have a cushion if he liked. But when Dan's mum wanted to change Dan's trousers, she forgot about being Mum and ran off so that he would follow. Dan's mum was cross and said would they please come back and stop being so naughty. When Dan looked as though he might be going to wee on the carpet, Lily put on the deep voice and offered to run and fetch the potty. She was just in time, too!'

Babies and young children generally behave according to how they see themselves

Behaving in character

On the whole, people behave 'in character'. In other words, what we do makes sense in terms of how we see ourselves (Curry and Johnson, 1990, pp. 27–8). When a person does something that seems 'out of character', the reason may be that the person sees him or herself differently from the way the rest of us do. Our knowledge and perception of other people is based on the evidence of what they do, what they say and how they look. Our self-concept is based on evidence, too, but how we see this is affected by the mirror process of how others see us. It is also affected by our ideas of what we *could* do if we chose – what we can imagine ourselves doing.

This works the other way around as well. We tend not to do things we do not think of ourselves as doing. 'I wouldn't dream of doing such a thing,' you might say, or, 'Nothing was further from my mind'. Although people sometimes surprise themselves by what they do, it is worth remembering that our minds work on a subconscious level for much of the time, and that subconscious wishes and needs can be even more powerful than conscious ones.

Self-concept in relation to behaviour

The idea that we tend to behave according to how we see ourselves seems at first rather a limited view. If we need to envisage doing something before we are likely to do it, how can we learn to behave in new ways? Of course, you only have to do something once, such as catching a ball or making someone laugh, to get the idea that you are now a person who catches balls and makes people laugh, and then you can do these things anytime (Erikson, 1950, p. 211). Sometimes this happens by chance, but often someone else says something like, 'Why don't you have a go, I know you can do it'. A possibility in someone else's mind suddenly becomes a possibility in our own. As Joanne said about Joe:

He thinks he's a clown so he makes us laugh . . . it all depends what he thinks.

One important way that children learn to behave in new ways is in pretend play. By pretending to be someone else, they can behave like that person (Light, 1979, pp. 41–61). The rules are strict:

'I am Mum today, so I can only do what Mum would do' or 'I am being the Bad Baby, so I can . . .!'

In their play, children often adopt characters from favourite television programmes or stories, and this can have a profound influence on their developing sense of self. They 'think themselves into role' as thoroughly as professional actors, but at a time when their own sense of identity is still in the making.

This 'trying on' of personality (remember we actually refer to children 'trying it on') is a wonderful, natural, safe way of exploring how to be acceptable – of rummaging about in the possibilities. Children 'try it on' with their important adults, as they do with each other. It is a way of trying out how to behave, without committing themselves; they are completely in control, ending the experiment at any moment by dropping the role. It also enables them to explore their reactions to painful and frightening situations – for instance violence or death – at the safer distance of one remove from reality. Children who have been able to do this are better able to manage those situations in real life.

How children see themselves and how they behave as a result of their self-perception are such complex and interrelated aspects of self that it is helpful to find a way of untangling the threads and considering them one at a time. Then it becomes possible to get an idea of what is happening to these threads in individual children. Curry and Johnson (1990, pp. 5–9) suggest using four areas: acceptance, power and control, about values, and competence.

Between child and mother, between child and other important people, between brothers and sisters and between friends, the factor of acceptance is at the heart of self-concept. Infants and young children are starting on the struggle for the second factor, power and control. This is not only about exerting control over their environment; it is also about achieving self-control. The third area, about values, refers to the child's developing concept of good and bad, right and wrong. The fourth area, competence, relates to the child's developing social, emotional, physical and cognitive skills, his or her ability to solve problems and the resulting sense of competence.

Much of the most influential work on the very early development of self-concept was carried out between 1950 and 1980. Although there has been a great deal of research and writing in relation to the brain and to the development of curricula, the earlier work on self-concept remains important today. It still appears that the development of behaviour and the development of self-concept are interdependent, and that in thinking about the development of one, we also need to think about the development of the other. Self-concept profoundly influences behaviour every-where – in families, in schools, in our world.

2

Being a key person

– DAD'S HOME! –

❝ *'We're home,' called Mum as she came through the door. She'd left Joe in his push-chair while she went into the kitchen to put the kettle on. Lily trailed in after her, holding Christina (that's her doll) by one leg, and looking hot and tired. It was Saturday and we'd been at the park nearly all afternoon. Lily always goes to the swings first, and now Mum pushes her really high, so the chains go slack at the top and the world stands still. She loves that. I never see her walk in the park, she always has to run, all the time.*

Mum went to get Joe out of his chair; and Lily took Christina into the back room. And guess what? There was her dad! He'd come home early and was sitting so quietly that we didn't know he was there. He didn't say a word, and nor did Lily – she just stood right in front of him and grinned at him, and he grinned back at her. I thought I'd be pretty happy if anyone was that pleased to see me!

'Hello, Tiger Lily!' He often calls her that, because of her bubbly gold hair; and because he says she's fierce. Once they were looking at themselves together in the bathroom mirror; with dad's black face and Lily's gold one.

'Definitely a tiger lily,' he said to her; grinning and tickling her to make her laugh.

'Been to the park?' he asked. 'What did you play on?' She told him all about the swing and about the girl who wouldn't go home when her brother told her to. (Though she didn't tell him that she wouldn't either, when Mum said.) Then he wanted to know about the rest of her day and what she had for lunch and if she'd enjoyed it. I think Lily's lucky to have him for her dad. He asked her all that stuff to let her know he hadn't forgotten her while he was out, and because he really wanted to know if she'd had a good day. Lots of dads ask because they want to know if you've been good or helpful or learned a lot. Then if you haven't, they don't want to know any more. ❞

Babies and young children need to be accepted by their important people

Holding

From the very earliest days, babies begin to build up their own internal ability to deal with their feelings. This ability is based on a growing feeling of internal strength, or wholeness, and a child's consciousness of being known and accepted is what helps that ability to grow (Bettelheim, 1987, pp. 146–65). Feelings of internal wholeness, and of disintegration, are reflected in the language we use to describe them. 'She's a "very together" person,' we might say, or 'I'm falling to pieces'.

Babies' actions often reflect their efforts to 'hold themselves together'.

> *Joe held the piece of orange firmly, first in his right hand, then in both. He put it very cautiously into his mouth and hastily removed it again after one tentative lick, screwing up his face as he did so. A second later, he tried again, this time tasting it for longer and screwing up his face less, as though he was getting used to the sharpness and really quite liked it. All this time he was holding it with both hands and looking at it carefully each time he took it out of his mouth. It seemed to make all the difference that he was holding something in both hands that also felt and tasted good in his mouth – as if the piece of orange was holding him together in some way, and without it he would fall apart and be miserable again.*

Sometimes the strain of 'holding themselves together' gets too much for babies and young children, and this is when important people can help. When they feel they are falling to pieces, they need a sense of being held, until they can manage again for themselves. There are various ways of giving this sense; it can come from physical action or from mental awareness. Who we are in relation to the child and where we are will dictate which ways are most appropriate. For a four-year-old at bed-time, a cuddle might be most appropriate; for the same four-year-old in the nursery setting, a pretend game inside a big cardboard box might be the answer; sometimes just not being forgotten is what is needed – the child needs to know that he or she is 'held' in the important person's mind.

Knowledge and acceptance

Young children need to feel accepted, but, alongside that acceptance, they need to feel known. In terms of reassurance, acceptance only works if it comes with knowledge, and knowledge only works if it comes with acceptance.

If we are accepted by someone who doesn't know us very well, we fear that once that person 'knows the worst', their acceptance may turn to rejection. If acceptance is to work as the basis of positive self-concept, it must be based on knowledge. On the other hand, it is not reassuring to be well known by someone when their acceptance is in doubt; to be rejected, at any stage in life, by an important person who knows us well is indeed devastating. This is why being known but not necessarily accepted feels so precarious.

Rejection is a kind of loss, and, right from day one, babies and young children experience other losses which are a normal part of life. They lose the safety of the womb, the comfort of the breast, the presence of important people: day after day, life is made up of a series of little losses, together with occasional major ones. This is not to say that life is miserable for babies; fortunately, they live very much 'in the present', and of course they gain things as well as losing them. But from the ego-centric viewpoint of the baby or young child, each loss represents a rejection. These rejections must be balanced by acceptance if the baby is to grow up feeling acceptable.

At the stage when children start to belong to groups outside the family, such as day-care or pre-school, possible rejection takes on new meaning. It has been shown that children remember experiences of rejection by their peers and teachers with painful clarity (Paley, 1992, pp. 33–6). It can be argued that our job as important adults in these settings should include efforts to guard against 'the habit of rejection', whatever its cause. For physical, temperamental or biographical reasons, some children seem to be particularly precarious in this respect; they need to know that they are acceptable in order to learn.

Power of important adults

It is the possibility of knowledge without acceptance, or acceptance without knowledge, that gives us such power over the children for whom we are responsible. Because we are 'important', it is possible for us to devastate children by withholding or withdrawing our acceptance. The closer we are to children, and the better we know them, the more powerful we become.

There is, however, the other side of this coin. As our knowledge of a child gradually grows, our acceptance of that child carries more and more conviction. Important people may have the power to devastate by rejection, but they have the corresponding power to support and build through their acceptance.

A doctor's success in helping a child to be well or a teacher's success in helping a child to learn – or, of course, a parent's success in doing both – is directly related to his or her knowledge about the child. Success is thought to depend on a good 'match', of medical treatment to the growing body or of learning experiences to the developing mind. It can be argued that there is another, completely different but equally significant reason for gaining as detailed a knowledge of a child as possible. This reason is related to the child's self-concept. We tend to use the knowledge of children which we have gained by being 'important people' to look after them and help them to learn. We may, in addition, offer it back to the child in the form of realistic acceptance. The greater the depth of knowledge, the greater will be the power of our acceptance. The injunction to 'know the child' can take on a deeper meaning.

– *MUM AND JOE* –

❛ *Sometimes I wonder why Mum loves Joe like she does. If he woke me up like that all night, I reckon I'd feel more like giving him away.*

Mum was playing a game with him the other day giving him little bits of bread-stick because he's dribbly and grumpy with his teeth. Then she remembered the chips were cooking, and when she started to go away and look at them, Joe really wailed. She's so tired I thought she'd be cross or take no notice, but she didn't. She came straight back, picked him up and gave him a huge hug. She said, 'You're an old softy aren't you?' and hugged him some more and then took him off to look at the chips with her.

I think she doesn't mind him needing her really; maybe she quite likes it. Perhaps that's why he cries every night, when he wakes up in his cot and wants to be in bed with Mum. He thinks he's in the wrong place, and the right place is with Mum. How can he learn to sleep all night without needing her? ❜

> **How babies and young children learn to see themselves is significantly affected by their growing knowledge of how to be acceptable to us**

Adult motivation

Babies begin to discover what sort of a person they are right from the first day. As this process of discovery is well under way before our words can be understood, babies develop other ways of understanding about what matters to their important people; they use their senses to gauge adult and sibling reactions. In our role as important adults, we cannot hide behind words. How we really feel and what we really think are the things with which babies are actually dealing.

If we accept that babies and young children are responding to what we really feel and think, we may feel the need to take an honest look at what we actually *do* mind about. This is probably easier said than done. Often feelings get lost, particularly if they are painful. However, feelings that have become subconscious still affect our reactions to things. Some parents, for instance, find it very difficult to have to listen to their baby crying; others may tolerate crying without feeling deeply upset, but, in spite of 'normal' development, are very anxious about whether the baby is feeding properly. Maybe these reactions are the results of parents' own early childhood experiences; our reactions may alter as we gain experience. In such situations, the responses the baby receives are likely to be governed by our own feelings, needs and priorities.

Parents who need their children to behave in certain ways may be responding to their own childhood. Those who did not experience an atmosphere of acceptance and tolerance as children were deprived; and they may continue, throughout their lives, to need and to seek the unconditional acceptance that their own parents did not give them at the time. In the balance of the generations, important people are in some ways mutual; the parents are important people for the child, but the child is also important for the adult.

So it can happen that, instead of receiving much needed unconditional acceptance, the baby's role is to recognise and accept the needs of one or both parents. As the parents' care is essential for the baby's existence, the baby begins to learn from the first day how to fit in with what the parents need. For example, a young child may learn to accept the food his parent gives him, not because he likes or needs it but because – probably unconsciously – he knows that the person on whom he depends for survival actually *needs* his acceptance in this way. It is 'safer' to eat up than to reject.

Unconscious messages

Some people may recognise their own childhood pattern in this description and may wonder if this means that the pattern inevitably repeats itself. The first step to take in answering this question is to try to do some 'self-watching', and notice the things that do seem, unaccountably or disproportionately, to matter very much. Then it becomes possible to think and talk about those things and to balance them with what we know about the unconditional acceptance that babies and young children need.

Even as we extend unconditional acceptance to babies and young children, they are still learning all the time about how we want them to behave, at different times and in a variety of places. In the author's study of the development of positive self-concept and learning skills (Roberts, 1993), one of the issues to emerge was connected with how parents *feel* about their children's behaviour. The parents' reactions were found to vary, depending on whether the setting was the home or somewhere outside it. At home, positive reactions related to personal characteristics, such as affection, helpfulness and happiness. When out in public, parents were unanimous in their feeling that what matters most of all is that children's behaviour should be 'socially acceptable'. There was a difference, in the parents' view, between ideally acceptable 'home' behaviour – affectionate, helpful and happy – and ideally acceptable 'out' behaviour – conforming, obedient, polite, sociable and sharing.

This raises questions about children's perceptions of appropriate behaviour when they go to school. It must be assumed that, initially at least, school is perceived, by both parents and children, as 'out'. This question will be considered in more detail in Chapter 9. Meanwhile, why should the parents have felt so very strongly about their children's public behaviour?

If we are unsure of our own worth, we have no secure basis for seeing ourselves as acceptable. Those who are unsure about themselves need constant confirmation of their worth. The more important our role as parent or carer is to us, the more we are liable to mind about other people's judgement of our ability in that role.

We tend to be judged, in relation to our ability as parents or carers, by the behaviour of the children in our care. And unless we are very secure in the knowledge of our worth as parents and carers, we need those children to behave in ways that 'do us credit', hence the parents' anxiety about their children's behaviour. However, happiness and the ability to learn – which were the main goals of the parents in the study mentioned above – do not happen as a result of the ability to conform and share, to be obedient, polite and sociable. In fact, early struggles to be socially acceptable are not generally happy experiences, nor are they always consistent with the ways in which successful early learning naturally takes place. Of course it matters that children learn to adapt to the society in which they live, and the child who persistently asks questions and is 'into everything' may in certain circumstances be thought to be behaving badly. But such behaviour is exactly what makes for successful learning. To accept and value and manage it will help the child to see him or herself as a learner, rather than as naughty.

– *LILY'S SUPERMAN* –

❝ *Dan came to play with Lily yesterday; all dressed up like Superman he was. His mum had lent him her lovely scarf, and it was wound around his shoulders. He marched straight into the hall and announced, 'I'm Superman,' to no one in particular. Then he went up to Lily gave her a great big shove and said, 'Lily' very fiercely right in her face. Lily looked indignant and went straight off to Mum to complain, but she had just opened her mouth and taken a breath when she stopped. She stood there in front of Mum, thinking for a moment, and Mum looked at her and waited. Then she surprised us all by saying very firmly 'Dan's here to play'. And off they went to the kitchen!*

It's a good thing Mum doesn't mind a bit of chaos. Lily and Dan spent the rest of the morning playing 'Superman and Superwoman'. They made a house under the table with cushions and bowls and an old blanket, and Lily's dolls had to be the babies. Joe wanted to be in the game too, but he didn't stay long because Lily and Dan were so bossy. They said he was one of the babies, and that he had to be in a baby's place and stay there, so after a while he got fed up and went off to look for Mum. When Lily and Dan wanted it to be dinner-time, Mum said they'd better have Super-Dinner and she gave them a packet of Lily's favourite Crunchies to share. In the end though Lily got fed up too. She said Dan wouldn't let her share out the Crunchies, and he kept pushing her around. Dan said Superman was supposed to be the boss, and then Mum stopped them arguing by saying that if they didn't come quickly, it would be too late to go to the park for a picnic. ❞

Babies and young children generally behave according to how they see themselves

Imaginative play

By their first birthday, babies are already showing signs of self-awareness in the form of imitative play in which they might pretend to drink from an empty cup or comfort a teddy bear (Curry and Johnson, 1990, p. 27). As they grow older, pretend play becomes increasingly important to them (Light, 1979, p. 41). Supporting children's imaginative play is crucial (Bruce, 1996). It is only by pretending to be another person that a child can explore what it would be like to be that sort of person, and this is what children need to do in order to make real choices about themselves in relation to other people. A child who is only ever allowed to be him or herself cannot begin to understand what it would be like to be another person. This is the gift that drama gives us, and children's pretend play is drama in a very real sense.

Babies and young children have an amazing capacity for observing and remembering. What Dad said to the dog, where Mum left the keys, how the builder smooths cement with a trowel and where you hid the special biscuits – these are all commonplace observations to children, along with details of gesture and intonation. Crucially important role models for pretend play come first and foremost from within the family: mummies and daddies, the baby, even the dog. Children will play these pretend games with 'modern dress' and a bare stage, if costumes and scenery are not available; but when we provide cardboard boxes for beds or a cooker, remnants of fabric for blankets, old cast-offs for dressing-up clothes, and a few other 'props', this not only adds another dimension to the play, but signals our acceptance and recognition of its importance.

As children's lives unfold and widen to include people and places outside the home, television programmes and stories in books, so their choice of role models for their pretend play widens too. The richer the variety and complexity of characters they have to choose from, the more they will benefit from this sort of play. Allowing and encouraging children's play gives them a safe way to explore and begin to understand themselves, the people in their world and the situations in which they find themselves.

POSTSCRIPT TO PART 1: BABIES FIRST

Living or working with young children?
Questions to think about . . .

Babies and young children need to be accepted by their important people

---

1. What are some of the things that parents and carers can do to make sure that a baby or young child feels accepted?

How babies and young children learn to see themselves is significantly affected by their growing knowledge of how to be acceptable to us

---

2. What characteristics and behaviours do you find particularly acceptable in young children? What is unacceptable to you? Why?

Babies and young children generally behave according to how they see themselves

---

3. Try watching a child very carefully, for about half an hour. What have you learned about that child's self-concept?

RECOMMENDED FURTHER READING

For sharing with children . . .

Waddell, M. and Benson, P. (1992), *Owl Babies*, **London, Walker Books**
'Once there were three baby owls: Sarah and Percy and Bill. They lived in a hole in the trunk of a tree with their Owl Mother'. This beautiful picture book is always a hit with small children, because they completely understand the plot. It's night-time, and Mum is out. Will she come back?

Ormerod, J. (1997), *Peek-a boo*, **London, The Bodley Head**
Babies love playing peek-a-boo, and this ingenious flap book is a winner. The pictures are enchanting, and the flaps are good and big so babies can easily get hold of them. With its 'snuggle down baby . . .' ending it makes a lovely going-to-sleep book, too.

. . . and for a good read

Gerhardt, S. (2004), *Why Love Matters: How Affection Shapes a Baby's Brain*, **London, Routledge**
With this book Sue Gerhardt has made a wonderful contribution to our understanding of the needs of babies. She writes about the fundamental importance of babies' first relationships, and how these early relationships affect the way the brain develops. This book is full of information about the latest findings in neuroscience, psychology and biochemistry, and – as the title indicates – is an extremely compelling and accessible read. In describing the links between early experiences and adult states, it shows very clearly why warm, responsive relationships are so important for babies.

PART 2

FUNDAMENTAL FEELINGS

3

Children's normal bad feelings

— CATS AND DUSTPANS —

❛I'm the lucky one just now. Lily likes me. I sat down on the floor to play with her the other day and straight away Toby (he's the cat) got on my lap and curled up so I couldn't move. Mum was there too, so she knelt on the floor and sat Lily on her lap, just opposite. Lily gazed and gazed at me so solemnly but when she looked at Toby on my lap, I was glad I wasn't him. After a bit, Toby got down and padded off past where Mum and Lily were, and as he went by, Lily grabbed his tail and pulled it really hard, laughing and looking at me! Mum was cross and told her to stop, so she let go with a flourish and went off to get the biscuit tin. When she'd got the lid off and had a good look inside, she came over to me, holding the tin out with a huge smile.

I was quite surprised that she was angry with Toby because he'd been on my knee. Usually it's Joe that makes Lily feel hurt and angry because he's got Mum. I remember when Mum was trying to feed Joe and help Lily with her play-dough all at the same time. Lily kept asking Mum to do things that needed two hands, so that she would have to put Joe down, and Mum kept managing it without stopping Joe's feeding. I felt sorry for Mum, trying to please everybody, and I felt really sorry for Lily too, because she was so desperate. In the end Lily gave up trying to empty Joe's mouth of Mum, and stuffed all the play-dough right into her own mouth instead — if you can't beat 'em, join 'em! And when Mum made her spit it out because it's not for eating, she threw it right across the kitchen. And Joe watched it all from the crook of Mum's arm, with that 'I've got the cream' smile.

Still, Joe doesn't have things all his own way. I remember when he crawled all the way from the far end of the sitting-room to play with the dustpan and brush. He had almost made it, when Mum swooped down and removed it to a safe place. Joe was so furious, he put his head down on the floor and really shouted. Two minutes later he wasn't allowed to play with the big pot of nappy cream either; so he shouted all over again. He must have thought we were following him around spoiling his fun on purpose.❜

As well as feeling love, it is normal for babies and young children to feel pain, anxiety and anger

Normal mixed feelings

'Don't worry . . . be happy . . .' goes the song. When a new baby is born, in whatever culture or situation, there are always worries mixed with the happiness, and adjustments to be made. As a baby grows into childhood, our job as important adults may become more and more challenging, sometimes even overwhelming. One of the most difficult things for us to manage is children's expressions of pain, anxiety or anger. If a baby or young child is still unhappy or angry even after we have done our best, we may feel exhausted, rejected – a failure.

When we think of normal 'bad' feelings, it helps to remember the normal 'good' feelings of love and pleasure which also make up our lives with babies and young children. Quite rightly, love and pleasure for children are often our first consideration; but if they are the *only* consideration, we run a risk by ignoring other, more negative, feelings.

Unavoidably, and in the normal course of events, babies and young children have a very great deal in their lives that hurts, that is worrying and that is infuriating. It would not be desirable, even if it were possible, to protect them entirely from these normal real-life experiences, as they represent a crucial source of learning. Consequently, we have to live with babies' and young children's expressions of pain, anxiety and anger. This can be made a great deal easier by understanding as much as possible about what these emotions may feel like for them.

Reasons for 'bad' feelings

What does it feel like for the child whose life is just beginning? To find some answers to this question, we can study our own 'important children' at home or work, as much and as carefully as possible. We can also learn from the writings of people who have studied other babies and young children.

Some experiences are common to all children. The abrupt emergence into a world after nine months in the womb is both a liberation and a stark shock. At birth, the freedom from the confines of the womb and birth canal is combined with the new effect of the full force of gravity, so that every movement requires both less and more effort than before. Gone are the familiar sights, sounds and sensations of the months before birth; suddenly the world is vast, bright, noisy, smelly and unknown. After the loss of the womb comes a different set of life-lines involving breathing, feeding, people and places. Every experience for the baby contains the possibility of pleasure, the probability of loss: the feed must end, the cuddle will not last forever, the nappy must be changed (Miller, 1992a). In small ways, the baby is learning to live with loss day by day. Some babies, on occasion, seem to find this quite overwhelming. A loved person goes out or the room looks different, and their world collapses.

Crying

Babies cry for a variety of reasons. D.W. Winnicott (1964, pp. 58–68) suggests that there are four normal kinds of crying. His first reason was that babies cry in order to feel that they are exercising their lungs. Winnicott suggests that pleasure can enter into crying as it can into any bodily function, and that this sort of crying is for satisfaction. Then there is the cry of pain: as well as indicating present pain, including hunger, this can signal painful memories or fear of pain.

Babies also cry with rage, and this ability to be angry with another person when things are not right is very important. Being in a rage is frightening for babies and young children because they feel destructive and dangerous; they need the experience of an adult who can tolerate that rage and not be badly hurt or destroyed by it. A calm response in the face of a tantrum gives the child confidence and reassurance about the possibility of accepting and managing those feelings. An adult who feels unable to tolerate a tantrum and tries to avoid one at all costs is confirming a child's fear that, in such a state, he or she is indeed destructive and dangerous, and that the damage cannot be mended.

The fourth type of crying that Winnicott outlines is that of grief: what he calls 'a song of sadness'. An infant's ability to cry from grief is as important as crying from rage, but more complex. Winnicott suggests that this sad crying is an early version of the ability to say 'sorry' and 'thank you', and that receiving the acceptance, sympathy and comfort that babies and children need in this state is much more valuable than teaching the words 'sorry' and 'thank you'.

In her book *Your Baby and Child* (2003, pp. 113–23), in the section 'Crying and comforting', Penelope Leach strongly disagrees with Winnicott's view that babies may cry for bodily satisfaction. She describes a range of situations that may cause babies to cry, with ways to help them. These include hunger, pain, over-stimulation, shock and fear, mis-timing, being undressed, feeling cold, jerks and twitches, lack of physical contact. The whole section is very helpful, for parents and carers who are struggling both with a crying baby, and with their own feelings as they try to manage and alleviate the baby's distress.

Underlying the routines of day-to-day living for most babies and young children is a strong determination to explore, to find out and to gain control. From birth, this 'need to know' is evident in their behaviour (Gopnik *et al.*, 1999). They listen and watch, they struggle to touch, to move, to taste – this is how they find out. Often these explorations are immensely satisfying, but the struggle to do all these things is also beset by frustrations, initially because of the limitations of their own physical ability, and later because often what they want is either incomprehensible or unacceptable to the adult who is in control. Frustrations, especially as a result of not being able to explore, are another major source of normal 'bad' feelings.

Brothers and sisters

Another cause for these normal 'bad' feelings can be brothers and sisters. Judy Dunn (1993, pp. 1–14) tells us that there are many variations in different settings and cultures about the ways in which children relate to each other and to adults. It is important not to make generalisations about such a very complex issue. It must also be clear to anyone who watches children in a variety of situations that very many children gain a great deal of love and pleasure from relationships with their brothers and sisters.

At the same time, however, there can be no doubt of the potential for normal 'bad' feelings between siblings. For a young child, the arrival of a new baby means that – however much is to be gained – the child who was the previous 'baby' will no longer enjoy the exclusive relationship that existed with the mother, but must give it up to someone else. This often coincides with weaning, which means losing the mother's breast and/or bottle as the main source of nourishment and cuddles. Of course, there is much to be said for being 'the grown-up one', but even so, the displacement from that special place with the mother can be hard to bear. There is much good advice from Penelope Leach (2003, pp. 422–9) on how an older sibling may be feeling at the birth of a new baby, and how to manage during the weeks around the birth, and for the first few months, in order to help that older child.

The 'built-in' difficulties in sibling relationships are not confined to the older child. In an earlier book (1984, p. 55), Judy Dunn writes of the predicament for the younger child:

> *If you grow up from four to ten years old with someone who knows you intimately, spends a great deal of time with you and relentlessly disparages and criticises you, while himself appearing effortlessly more capable and successful, surely this experience will have a profound effect on your sense of your own value and efficacy, and will affect your behaviour with others outside the home.*

Of course, this is not true for all sisters and brothers, but it indicates the ordinary psychological reactions that can result from normal bad feelings at such close quarters.

– MIXED-UP LILY –

❝ *I think Lily is often fierce with the cat because it's safer than being fierce with people, especially Joe. It isn't only when she's angry with Joe, though. There was that time when their dad went away for a fortnight, and after about ten days, I think she was afraid he wasn't coming back. I suppose it's a long time when you're that young. That was when she got really quiet and she wouldn't let Mum out of her sight, but she was wild with the cat, pulling his tail and shouting 'Eat!' at him when he was eating already. It's safer to kick the cat, isn't it? The grown-ups might not love her if she kicks them, especially not if she does it to Joe; and that's what she's afraid of.*

Lily's such a mixed-up kid when it comes to Joe. The other day she was playing with the Duplo and she kept sweeping the pieces off the table so that they landed on Joe's head, but the next moment she handed him Old MacDonald, which is one of her favourites. Sometimes she plays like she's two people, one laughing and distracting and finding toys, and the other pushing and squeezing and bumping. I think it's great that she plays with him at all, after everything he's taken over from her. I think she really loves him, and it makes her feel better when she can manage the bad feelings enough to make room for the good ones – then she knows she's a good sister. She doesn't only play with him because she knows Mum will be pleased – sometimes she really wants to play with him as well, and then she feels good. **'**

Denied pain, anxiety and anger all undermine positive self-concept – these feelings are hard to acknowledge and manage unless they are recognised by others as normal and acceptable

Acknowledging 'bad' feelings

We seem to spend a lot of time and energy denying pain, fear and anger and trying to eliminate these emotions from our lives. We may avoid the causes, by not speaking to someone or withdrawing from a situation. Alternatively, we may try to 'pass on' our feelings to someone else, for instance by being irritable with someone who had nothing to do with the reason for our feelings. Often, this person will be someone in whose love we have confidence and with whom it is therefore 'safe' to be irritable. So when things get bad, our inclination is often to keep out of the way or, if we can't do that, to 'dump' our feelings on the nearest 'safe' person.

Babies and young children quickly begin to develop the ability either to avoid pain, fear and anger (requiring some form of anticipation) or to pass on feelings (requiring the ability to communicate, although not necessarily in spoken language). As adults, we tend to encourage this ability: we say things like 'Don't cry', 'Come on, there's no need to be scared', and 'Will you stop making that noise!' Or maybe we use distractions, 'Look, what's your teddy doing on the floor?' and 'Would you like a biscuit?'

However, there are grounds for recognising the great importance, for babies and children, of experiencing their true feelings and coming to know themselves (Miller, 1979, pp. 19–29). Children who have not been allowed to express their negative feelings may be in danger of a kind of emotional helplessness. Feelings do not cease to exist simply because they are denied; instead, what tends to happen is that they become all the more powerful for having been ignored. Emotional development is about learning how to accept and manage feelings, both positive and negative, and how to respond appropriately.

Cognitively, evasions and distractions are unhelpful too. Children who have been encouraged to think about something else every time something goes wrong are likely to be low on concentration and persistence in problem-solving situations.

For babies and young children, acceptance of *all* sorts of feelings is possible if they are given enough opportunities to be themselves. However, the need to accept something before it is possible to deal with it – whether the 'something' is an emotion, a person or a situation – must be one of the most unrecognised and unpractised essentials of human relationships. We need to realise that, in order to resolve a situation, we must accept its existence.

Sometimes, however, the unconscious needs of parents prevent children from achieving this acceptance. In the author's study (Roberts, 1993, pp. 67–74), parents were asked about their feelings in relation to their children's behaviour. In answer to the question, 'What does your four-year-old do that makes you feel particularly rejecting and disapproving?', the almost unanimous answer was that forms of verbal protest are the hardest aspect of children's behaviour for their parents to accept. It may be that, in our responses to children, we do accept their feelings, sympathising and trying to resolve the situation; or perhaps we try to refuse to allow the crying, complaints, arguments and quarrels; or maybe we grit our teeth and take no notice. Probably most parents have tried all these, but common sense and observation would suggest that, when children cry, complain, argue or quarrel, we 'important adults' usually do our best to get them to stop.

We would all like children to learn to deal with their feelings so that there is less crying, complaining, arguing and quarrelling. But that is only possible if children are allowed to *have* the feelings in order to work on them. If we, as 'important adults', feel rejecting and disapproving when children express their negative feelings, the children soon learn to hide them, which makes it impossible to try to accept and resolve them. Hidden feelings are always liable to re-emerge, out of control, as in Black's (1991) splendid poem 'The Red Judge'. Feelings that have been accepted and thought about are generally more manageable. This is how children begin to think about right and wrong.

The cycle of loss

As discussed in Chapter 1, children need their important people's acceptance; so, if 'bad' feelings are not acceptable, they must be hidden if the child is not to risk losing the most important thing in the world – the acceptance of the important adult. Miller

(1979, pp. 21–3) describes the way in which many adults actually need to be accepted by their children, because of their own parenting. This may be why it is so hard for many of us to tolerate children's protests: when a baby goes on crying in spite of our best efforts, or when a two-year-old has a tantrum, there is a part of us that feels rejected.

Here is what seems to be a frequent cycle of events:

- First, a child feels the need to learn to hide unacceptable 'bad' feelings.
- Second, the child's developing self-perception grows to exclude those hidden feelings.
- Third, the self-concept which has excluded those 'bad' feelings loses them altogether into the subconscious (but losing something does not mean that it ceases to exist).
- Fourth, the growing child is thereby deprived of the opportunity to accept and come to terms with the feelings of pain, fear and anger that are a normal part of early childhood; instead, those feelings remain a dead weight in the subconscious, beyond control.
- Fifth, in adulthood these children may find it hard to manage feelings of pain, anxiety or fear, and anger. They may avoid situations involving those feelings, may consistently need to 'dump' them on others, or may respond very violently. They may also require unconditional acceptance from their own children, because the need for acceptance has not yet been met.

When these things happen, the cycle starts again for the sake of the needy adults. We need to find ways of breaking this repeating pattern, so that our children grow into adults who are better able to understand and manage their own feelings.

– MUM'S MAGIC –

❝ That time when the kids' dad was away, Lily was struggling to make sense of why he wasn't there. She was really hurting because he was gone. She was confused and sad. I thought Mum did a clever thing to help her: she got out the photos and helped Lily to sort out all the family ones so that she could look at her dad and they could talk about him. After they'd looked at the photos, they talked about what he was doing and when he was coming back, and then he seemed to be real again for Lily. Mum said she missed him, too. Lily was better for a bit after that.

Mum's really good at understanding when they feel sad because someone's missing. She knows how they feel, even if she can't bring the person back. She's not so understanding when Lily's angry, though; Lily wants to hit people and throw things when she's angry – of course, she mustn't, but even her wanting to do it makes Mum cross. When it's Joe, he just roars, and Mum always wonders what's the matter. She looks at him really carefully, and then he seems to feel safer. She still always tries to stop him roaring though. Can't say I blame her – who wants hitting and throwing and roaring?

But it's funny, as soon as she does sympathise they stop anyway; it's when she takes no notice that they go on and on. ❯

Babies and young children can manage pain, anxiety and anger more easily if they know that other people accept and sympathise with how they feel

---

Containment

Most of us have experienced the relief of having someone listen with complete attention while we explain about something that is upsetting us. Even if that person is unable to be of any practical help, the fact that he or she is willing to accept how we feel can be helpful, provided that person is not drawn in to feeling as we do. Calm acceptance by someone else of how we feel helps us to accept and deal with our feelings and to think about appropriate responses; whereas, for instance, panic-stricken or angry acceptance tends to 'stoke up' our own fear or anger. The same can be true for babies and young children.

'Containment' is a helpful term for the way in which a mother (or mother-figure) can accept and hold a child's pain, anxiety or anger at a stage when the child is finding it overwhelming. Containment also involves not losing those feelings for the child, but making them accessible later in a form in which the child can deal with them. This is what Mum was helping Lily to do when they were looking at the photographs.

The way in which mothers ensure that the distance between themselves and their children is not too great in times of difficulty is a primitive aspect of maternal care-giving described by Bowlby (1969, pp. 409–510). Physical 'holding' – previously referred to in Chapter 1 – is often accompanied by a kind of mental holding, sometimes referred to as containment. These ideas are akin to Bowlby's theory of attachment, which has been helpfully elaborated by Holmes (1993).

Erikson (1950, p. 200) reminds us that adults, when traumatised, tend to solve their tension by 'talking it out', and writes of 'the protective sanction of an understanding adult'. He suggests that for children, 'playing it out' with the undivided attention of an understanding adult is the most natural self-healing measure childhood affords.

It is important that, alongside nourishing and sharing the love and pleasure that children need, we also accept normal bad feelings. However, acceptance of 'bad' feelings does not have to involve unconditional acceptance of 'bad' behaviour (see Chapter 8).

Experiencing manageable feelings of loss, pain and frustration is most important. Growing up involves coming to terms with these things. We cannot hope to help children to manage their pain, fear and anger unless we are willing to try to understand their feelings. D.W. Winnicott (1964, p. 186) suggests that parents need enlightenment about underlying causes. We cannot hope to understand feelings unless we are willing to accept that the feelings exist and that they are important. The key is acceptance.

4

Adults accepting bad feelings

– THE BISCUIT BATTLE –

'Joe is so cross. He's cross with all of us, but especially with Mum. He's being a real pain in the night, always climbing into their bed and wanting to be fed. Mum says she's beginning to feel like a walking dummy, and it's time to sort Joe out. That's why Joe is so cross with her, because for once Mum's not doing exactly what he wants. When things went wrong before, he used to sound all despairing and abandoned, and it made you want to give him a huge cuddle; but now that he's angry, it's as if he doesn't want us, and that really hurts.

Today there was a big fuss about biscuits; Joe wasn't just pointing or whinging, he was being really bossy. Mum had already given him two, and he hadn't even eaten the second one. When she said, 'No, two is quite enough,' he shrieked and flung himself backwards. When she tried to pick him up and distract him, he went on throwing himself around and took absolutely no notice of anything she tried.

Mum was really patient with him until Lily came in, but the first thing Lily said was, 'Can I have a biscuit?' I don't know if she knew that was what Joe was fussing about, but she might have, and they often gang up on Mum now. Anyway, Mum said, 'No you can't,' really crossly, and Lily was wailing, 'But I'm hungry', and Mum nearly dropped Joe when he went all stiff and flung himself backwards again. Then the phone rang, only the two of them were making such a noise you could hardly hear it. Mum just dumped Joe on the floor and told Lily to go in the kitchen while she answered it. You'd think Mum had been knocking them about, the noise they were making.

Anyway the minute Mum answered the phone, she asked the person to hang on. Then she went straight and fetched the biscuits and put them on the floor by Joe, so Lily could reach them too. That shut them up! Mum told me afterwards that it was Lily's new nursery on the phone and she didn't know what they'd think if they heard the children crying like that. Then she said something about Joe winning yet again, and he'd better not make a fuss like that at Gran's.

Mum says she hates it when Joe's furious and resentful, and partly what she hates are her own feelings when he's like that. She says it makes her feel useless and *unwanted and also like hurting him back, and then she feels ashamed of herself for even feeling like that. I've noticed that she gets extra busy when that happens, rushing about so she hasn't got time to think. It wouldn't be so bad if she wasn't so tired; she says she can't remember what it's like not feeling tired. I used to think it would be wonderful to have a baby like Joe, but now I'm not so sure. I'd have to be strong enough to love him even when he was being a little monster. That's what their dad calls him sometimes – 'little monster' – but he mostly says it in such a loving voice; it's only now and then he sounds as if he means it.* **'**

As well as feeling love, it is normal for babies and young children to feel pain, anxiety and anger

Uses and abuses of distraction

This mixture of feelings may be further complicated when we consider our children's feelings alongside our own. We can look at not only our reactions to those of our 'important children', but also our reactions to our own feelings. It may be that sometimes we take our love and pleasure for granted, not acknowledging how we feel to the people concerned. In the study about self-perception already mentioned (Roberts, 1993), the children thought that what their parents most approved of at home – as well as outside the home – was obedience, politeness and conformity. However, the parents said that – at home – they placed most value on affectionate behaviour, with a willingness to learn being almost as important as 'social acceptability'.

Somehow those parents were accepting their children's love and affection without letting them know how much it meant. The study showed a sample of children struggling to be obedient and polite in order to gain their parents' approval, when what the parents said they wanted most was hugs and cuddles. Dealing with normal 'good' feelings involves acceptance and acknowledgement too.

It is hard for children to deal with feelings of frustration, pain and loss unless we, their important adults, are willing to acknowledge the existence of those feelings. Very often, however, it is much easier to distract a child – or indeed ourselves – from those feelings than to accept them and think what to do about them. There is no doubt that distraction can be an extremely useful strategy (as used by Mum on page 38). But it can sometimes mean not only that you will 'live to fight another day' but also that on another day there *will* be a fight. Unfortunately, the more practice children have at such battles, both at home and at school, the better they get at them; and the longer their negative feelings go unacknowledged and unresolved, the more entrenched they become.

Dealing with our own feelings

What about our own feelings as 'important adults'? Many adults were expected to hide their fear and anger in childhood; if this was the case, and if displays of affection seemed to go unnoticed, how does it feel when our 'important children' want to display their feelings? People who, in the past, have had to develop ways of keeping their feelings to themselves, may find it especially difficult to acknowledge and accept the feelings of others, including children.

Returning to our own feelings, it can be hard to accept that sometimes we may be so tired, anxious or frustrated that we feel like hurting a child. The danger is that, if we do not accept that occasionally it is normal to *feel* like that, it becomes difficult to control those feelings or to deal with them appropriately. There are two steps to take:

- to look beyond how we feel, to why we feel like that;
- to make a distinction between how we feel, and what we do about it.

This distinction is discussed further in Chapter 8.

Referring back to the 'cycle' described in Chapter 2, it is imperative that we learn how to accept our 'important children's' feelings – both positive and negative – so that they grow up more able to deal with their own feelings and the feelings of others. For many parents, teachers and citizens, there is a sharp awareness of the ever-increasing need for greater acceptance and understanding between people and between groups. Here is a way to halt the escalating tendency to confrontation and violence; a way in which, in our families, our schools and our society, we might move towards a more peaceful world.

– LILY IN CONTROL –

❛ *Lily is trying hard to keep Joe in his place, and it's a real battle. When he was just a baby at least she knew where he was; now he's all over the place. I love the way she invents games to tie him down. Yesterday they had this game under the table, and Lily said Joe's place had to be right at the back in the corner and he wasn't allowed to move! I was really surprised how long he stayed there.*

Lots of the toys Lily loves these days are about fastening things together or putting things in their right places. She's got a special doll with lots of buttons and zips and things – I think it's supposed to be for teaching her how to manage her own clothes, but she loves it because she can tie it up tight, just like she's trying to tie Joe up tight. I wonder if the toy shops would sell more of those dolls if they were labelled 'This doll makes children feel better about their baby brothers and sisters' instead of 'This doll teaches children to manage their own clothes'.

Lily likes strapping dolls into her buggy and she puts them to bed very firmly too. I suppose there's a bit of her that knows that it's not kind to Joe, wanting to get rid of him or wanting him to stay a baby for ever in a safe place where he can't take things from her. She can't help feeling like that, but she knows Mum and their dad don't like it, so she pretends.

Mum understands, though. Yesterday when they had the game under the table, Joe cried in the end, because Lily wouldn't let him out. Mum had to rescue him and give him a cuddle and she was quite cross with Lily for what she had done. But I saw her giving Lily a cuddle as well afterwards and she was saying something to Lily about Joe being a nuisance. What Lily said shows how mixed up she feels about him. Instead of being glad that Mum understands, she said, 'No, he's not!' and started arguing about it!

Denied pain, anxiety and anger all undermine positive self-concept – these feelings are hard to acknowledge and manage unless they are recognised by others as normal and acceptable

---

Siblings

It is clear from listening to the discussions of parents and people who work with children that it is common for adults to be concerned about whether, and how much, sisters and brothers love or hate each other. Many studies suggest that children often feel both love and hate at once, with friendly co-operation on the one hand and rivalry on the other. Dunn (1993, pp. 113–17) says that the brothers and sisters under five in her study who frequently entered into conflict were also found to be more likely to attempt to share, help and co-operate. According to Dunn, it appears that there is a wide range of differences between pairs of brothers and sisters, and that some pairs are both quarrelsome and friendly playmates, others are low on both negative and friendly dimensions, while other pairs are high on one or other dimension.

The general message from these studies seems to be that there are no obvious 'norms'. Relationships between brothers and sisters are varied and complicated, and raise a host of questions for us all. In different cultures, for instance, are variations in parenting significant in the way that relationships develop between siblings? Or is the basis of early relationships rooted in realities which cross different cultures? It seems that there are no straight answers to these questions. Although many studies have shown negative, hostile aspects of sibling relationships, more attention is now being paid to the way in which brothers and sisters are very often 'attached' to each other and to the ways in which they share thoughts and jokes, fantasies and playthings – often as equal partners.

It is entirely normal for brothers and sisters to play well together *and* to ignore each other, to agree *and* to argue, to love *and* to hate each other. These things are the basis of much early learning. This is not to say that 'only' children are disadvantaged. They have the benefit of their unique position and a longer period with an uninterrupted pattern of relationship with their parents; although they may need to develop certain social skills later, in the wider context of nursery, playgroup or school.

— *LISTENING TO LILY* —

❛*I think Lily's getting ill – maybe it's the flu I had last week. When Mum was getting her dressed this morning, she was really worried about having her hair brushed. Usually she doesn't mind much, but today she was crying about it. Mum got round it by saying she was sorry, but they really had to do it, and how about a story afterwards? Lily said 'No . . . yes!' and then she was really patient so that was all right. Mum always keeps her side of the bargain, so Lily knew it was worth it.*

The old lady who's just moved in down the road dropped in to see Mum this morning, and Lily wanted to show her the little camel she got from her dad last week. After the lady had looked at it, Lily wanted to go next door and show it to George and Kathleen. George is usually in the garden, and Kath always lets her have sweeties. Mum said no about this (we couldn't go when the lady was here) and Lily suddenly cried really loudly. It wasn't to get her own way but just because she wanted to go and knew she couldn't. It was just like the way she's suddenly sick when she's ill, except she was throwing up her feelings instead of her breakfast!

She was hanging on round Mum's neck while she was crying, and Mum was saying things like, 'I'm sorry' and 'Never mind' and rocking her. After a bit that seemed to work, and she stopped, and went off to play with the camel. It reminded me of when she was little and she burst a balloon right in her face by biting it; she was really frightened, but Mum was down on the floor with her straight away after the bang, and when she saw that Mum wasn't frightened, she decided maybe it wasn't so awful after all. Mum has to be there, thinking about her though; it doesn't work if she just takes no notice.

It's harder for Mum when Lily's angry. That time when Lily first went to Dan's mum all day, Mum went away quickly because she really didn't want to hear Lily fussing. Dan's mum said Lily had been fine all day but when Mum came back she was awful; she shouted and screamed and wouldn't put her coat on or do anything. In the end, Mum had to carry her home still screaming, and after Lily was asleep that night, I heard her tell their dad that she didn't know what was worse – feeling furious with Lily for making such a fuss in front of everybody, or feeling bad about not listening to her in the morning. Their dad said there is no point hanging about, if you're going to go, then go; but Mum said she thought Lily wouldn't have been like that if she'd been a bit sympathetic first, instead of just dumping her. It's when Mum takes no notice of how she feels that she minds.

Anyway after the lady had gone home this morning, Lily said she was tired, so Mum made her a bed on the old sofa downstairs with a blanket and a pillow. She's been asleep ever since, and we're all creeping around whispering. It's lucky Joe still sleeps in the morning. **?**

Babies and young children can manage pain, anxiety and anger more easily if they know that other people accept and sympathise with how they feel

Verbal protest

The hardest form of protest to deal with seems to be verbal protest. If a child is physically hurting another, or throwing things dangerously, we don't have to think too hard about our response; we need to stop the child's action, although we may have to think *how* to stop it. But verbal protest is more complicated.

Parents say that one of the most infuriating things to listen to is whinging. Should we take no notice? Try and be patiently understanding? Shriek with irritation? Or possibly all three in quick succession? Argument is another version of verbal protest that tends to 'wind us up'. It is very hard to win an argument effectively, even with a small child, without giving it your whole attention, which may indeed be exactly what the child is asking for. Other aspects of verbal protest, such as anger, rudeness and 'unrepentance', are liable to feel like rejection to the listener; rejection is something even the most balanced person finds hard to bear.

For those people who were not allowed to protest as children and may not have had much practice since, verbal protest may be particularly hard both to listen to and to make. For them, it is more difficult to appreciate its value for the developing child and thus to tolerate it. People who were denied this way of accepting and dealing with their own feelings may not yet have found ways to accept, understand and deal with the sort of emotions that children's verbal protest evokes. In our role as important adults, we need to look for ways to break this circle. Some suggestions are made in the last section of this chapter.

Changes for children

As growing babies and children are learning to manage the changes in themselves, they also encounter a variety of changes in the world around them. Some of these changes may seem small to us, like growing out of the high-chair and sitting on an ordinary one, or an older brother or sister starting school and therefore being out all day, but these things are major events for the young child. Other changes that may happen are major ones by any standards, such as a new baby, moving house, mum going to work or parents separating: these changes inevitably bring a host of lesser ones in their wake.

Of course, not all changes are bad, and a manageable amount of change is creative; but children get plenty of it in the normal course of events. As adults we know how stressful it feels when several big things in our lives are changing at once, and we don't feel quite in control of anything. This sensation is worth remembering when young children are faced with several major changes, or even one. Sometimes we are puzzled and worried by a child's behaviour, not realising that, for instance, moving house so that Gran comes to live with the family, as well as a new start at primary school, will have added up to 'a lot to cope with'.

One problem at a time

Usually there's not much to be done to avoid these changes, but sometimes it is possible to do something about the timing of them, from the child's point of view. It helps to aim for *manageable* change and to take things bit by bit. For instance, if Gran arrived a little while *after* the move to the new house, and if that move could be made a few weeks *after* the start of term, and if the reception teacher knows about what is happening at home, then those few months might contain a series of positive experiences for the child, rather than one long, overwhelming one.

This principle of 'one thing at a time' is a useful one to bear in mind if parents are separating. Children's parents, home, friends and school are four main areas of their lives. While the parent aspect is altering, it is important to try and keep the other three areas as unchanged as possible for a while.

Fathers

Much of this book may seem to focus on mothers, and it may appear like that because much of the subject matter – feelings and what to do about them – has traditionally been seen as 'women's territory'. We need to recognise and accept the crucial role of fathers as 'important people' also. A father can play so many roles, each one a different expression of his love for his child. John Lewis-Stempel's anthology of fatherhood (2001) is a timely reminder of the joys and pains of fatherhood down the centuries.

Expectations of and by fathers have changed radically during recent decades; the idea of the father as an occasional 'stand-in mother' has given way to a wider recognition of 'fathering' as separate and complementary to 'mothering', and of equally crucial importance in a distinct way. Both in their relationship with the mother as a co-parent and in their relationship directly with the child, fathers have a special part to play in the development of the child. For boys, the influence of the father as a role model (what he does rather than what he says) is very considerable, and it is the same with girls and their mothers (Holditch, 1992, pp. 6–65). This does not mean that fathers are less important to girls, or mothers to boys, but that the role modelling, although also important, may be less influential.

Accepting feelings, therefore, is an important issue for both parents as role models. Not only will girls *and* boys have a greater chance of learning to accept and manage how they feel, but they may be more likely to approach others, including their own children, in an accepting way.

Brazelton (1992, p. 423) writes:

All of the studies that measure the increasing involvement of fathers in their babies' care-taking point to the gains in the babies' development. Not only do school-aged children demonstrate significant gains in their IQ in families where the father was involved with them as infants, but they show more sense of humour, longer attention spans, and more eagerness for learning. These studies show that fathers who are available to their children enrich the child's self-image, and they also suggest that his involvement contributes to more stable family support for the child. A recent study demonstrates that father involvement gives the adolescent a surer sense of her inner 'focus of control' – the ability to resist peer pressure because she is sure of her own values.

The role of 'important person' is becoming increasingly complicated as new opportunities arise, dilemmas multiply and the world changes around us. As the pressures both in employment and in unemployment increase, and as the separation and divorce rates rise, more and more parents are having to make conscious decisions about spending time with their children. It is clear that, whatever the pattern of the family, fathers' involvement matters for children.

Easing distress

Here are three suggestions for making life easier when hurt, anxious or angry children need us at home, in nursery, playgroup or school:

1 Young children tend to carry on complaining or protesting until they feel they have been heard, even if it takes all day. A few minutes at the beginning of the protest spent listening carefully may be minutes well spent. Even if the problem remains unsolved, you may have stemmed the flow by accepting that the child's grievance is genuine, at least to him or her.
2 Bearing in mind that babies and children can manage better if they know that we accept how they feel, it's worth being openly sympathetic; adding sympathy to acceptance often reduces the pain, even if we cannot actually solve the child's problem. This does *not* mean that you have to do what the child wants, unless that is what you decide.
3 If sympathy seems impossibly inappropriate (and it probably only works if it is genuine), a little detachment may help. This involves allowing the protest to con-

tinue while watching and listening really carefully. As babies' and young children's 'unreasonable' behaviour is almost always reasonable from *their* point of view, it may be possible to see or hear something with which to sympathise after all. Then suggestion number 2 has a chance.

If these suggestions seem to make no difference, do not be entirely discouraged. Very often children, and adults too, are profoundly affected by the close attention of another person, even if they cannot show it. Sympathetic acceptance certainly feels better than being ignored, even if the child is unable to acknowledge it at the time.

Miller (1992b, p. 52) writes:

> *The process whereby a child can convey distress to an understanding and receptive adult and be made to feel better is a most important one for the child's emotional development. As everyday experience tells us, 'a trouble shared is a trouble halved'. You cannot turn back the clock and make a child not have fallen over, and you cannot really abolish the fact that this gave him a nasty shock and a sore knee that will take time to mend. But you can understand how bad he feels, you can listen to his distress and you can absorb it. There will be times, of course, where the child is on his own. There will be times when grown-ups are busy or unsympathetic, or when they will deny or make light of his pain. But if he has enough experience of times when someone can bear his pain or worry with him, his own resources to bear distress will increase. He will feel as though he carries around in his memory and his imagination, consciously and unconsciously, helpful figures who will stand by him in his hour of need. This is how children themselves learn to be helpful and sympathetic.*

It is sometimes suggested that the best way to deal with a temper tantrum is to ignore it. The alternative of sympathetic acceptance may have more to recommend it. Sharing children's frustration or distress with them in a calm way, without fuss or panic, is one of the most effective things that 'important people' can do to help children grow up feeling good about themselves and other people.

POSTSCRIPT TO PART 2: FUNDAMENTAL FEELINGS

Living or working with young children?
Questions to think about . . .

> As well as feeling love, it is normal for babies and young children to feel pain, anxiety and anger

1. In your experience, what are the most common causes of pain for babies and young children? What causes anxiety? What makes them angry?

> Denied pain, anxiety and anger all undermine positive self-concept – these feelings are hard to acknowledge and manage unless they are recognised by others as normal and acceptable

2. How can we let children know that pain, anxiety and anger are normal for us too, without undermining their security?

> Babies and young children can manage pain, anxiety and anger more easily if they know that other people accept and sympathise with how they feel

3. What can we do to show very young children that we accept and sympathise with their difficult feelings?

RECOMMENDED FURTHER READING

For sharing with children . . .

Wishinsky, F. and Thompson, C. (1998), *Oonga Boonga: Big Brother's Magic Words*, London, Picture Corgi
Magic words or a magic relationship? Baby Louise keeps on crying, and all day no one can help until her brother Daniel comes home from school with the magic words. But they don't work for anyone else . . . this wonderful book is full of love and humour.

Campbell, R. (1982), *Dear Zoo*, London, Macmillan Children's Books
This little book combines many things that greatly appeal to young children: a selection of animal favourites, flaps, excitement, rhythm and repetition. *Dear Zoo* has become a classic – it even has a happy ending!

. . . and for a good read

Dunn, J. (2004), *Children's Friendships: The Beginnings of Intimacy*, Oxford, Blackwell Publishing
In his introduction to this fascinating book Jerome Bruner says Judy Dunn shows that the principal things that young children who are friends share, is pretending: pretend games, pretend stories, pretend actions, pretend heroes and villains. This rings as true here as it does in Vivian Gussin Paley's book (recommended in Part 5). Dunn tells us that children who are securely attached to their mothers make higher quality friendships, and gives us many magical and thought-provoking glimpses of such friendships in action.

PART 3

ABOUT OTHER PEOPLE

5

Children living with other people

– LILY NEEDS HER DOLLS –

❛When I got home yesterday they were all out. I looked round the back but the garden was empty. Lily's and Joe's toys and shoes and clothes were lying all over the grass, and it was very hot and quiet. I sat on the swing and thought about being Lily. Sometimes she swings on the swing for ages. I wonder what she thinks about.

I heard her feet first. She came running round the corner of the house, with Mum and Joe just behind. Mum looked really hot and loaded down, carrying Joe with one arm, two dolls in a basket under the other and the picnic bag over her shoulder, too. They said they'd come to find me, and would I come with them to the park? Lily said everyone must go – Mum and Joe and her dolls and me.

'We'll just leave your dolls inside, they're too heavy to carry as well as Joe.' Mum was tired.

'Want my dollies to come.'

Mum's voice was patient.

'They're really too heavy – they'll be quite all right until we come back.'

'Want my dollies.' Her voice was even more determined than before.

'I really think they'd be better here.' Mum was nearly at the back door.

Lily's voice rose.

'I want everybody. I want my dollies too. I'll carry them.'

Mum turned around and came back. Without a word, she took them both out of the basket and gave them to Lily. Then she put the empty basket down on the grass, humped up Joe on her hip and led the way to the front gate. Silently Lily handed the dolls to me and followed her.

We walked down the road with Lily running ahead at a steady trot, with her head slightly down. After a little way she turned around and came back to us, drooping.

'Want a carry.'

Mum bent down and picked her up with her free hand, so that she had one on each hip. I offered to help, but Mum said they both seemed to need her at the moment, and she was quite well balanced with one on each side! Mum doesn't seem to mind things if Lily has a good reason, even if we don't know what the reason is.❜

'Unreasonable' behaviour is almost always reasonable from the point of view of the baby or young child doing it

Other people's point of view

The opinion that 'unreasonable' behaviour can be reasonable, depending on your point of view, partly concerns the behaviour of other adults and children from the child's perspective, and partly concerns the child's own behaviour.

Babies and very young children are not generally able to think about another person's point of view, unless they can imagine themselves 'in that person's shoes' (Donaldson, 1978, pp. 17–31). They cannot understand what it's like to be an adult, although ideas are beginning to form as they gain experience in a variety of situations. Their ability to do this has been the starting-point of much debate (Bruner and Haste, 1987).

The tantrums of three-year-olds and the career choices of four-year-olds give some indication of how far they have to go! When Lily insisted on taking her dolls to the park, she didn't know how hot and tired Mum felt. She just knew that she needed her dolls for playing in the park. Yet often in matters that are directly relevant to them, young children show an awareness of what it's like to be the other person. Three- and four-year-olds sharing out biscuits usually display a very strong sense of justice! Sometimes a parent, at a loss as to the cause of the two-year-old's distress, will turn to the four-year-old for an explanation. Dunn (1988, p. 38) explores the extent of young children's early sensitivity to other people's feelings.

Generally, there is a reason for how someone is behaving which makes sense to *them* (Bannister and Fransella, 1986, p. 65). Mum could have refused to pick Lily up on the way to the park, on the grounds that Lily had had a rest after lunch and couldn't really be tired; or she might have argued that Lily needn't be jealous of Joe, because Mum had carried Lily just as much when she was little, so she's had her turn. But that wouldn't have helped Lily to feel better. She just wanted a carry, and Mum knew that her wanting wasn't going to be reasoned away.

In discussing ways of handling aggression towards other children, Goldschmied and Jackson (2004, pp. 201–21) make the following important point about the needs of the aggressor:

> *Although it is the child who has got hurt to whom we give our immediate attention as we intervene to stop the conflict and comfort the victim, it is important to notice how the aggressor is looking, which is often pretty unhappy. How we then relate to him (or her) also needs our understanding; there is little point in asking 'Why did*

you hit her?', a question to which a child is most unlikely to give an answer which has any meaning. Some kind of statement is more likely to be of help to the child, such as 'I know you're angry but you can't get what you want by hitting her – let's see what the trouble is'. In this way, the feeling is recognised but it is made clear that the action is not acceptable.

The sort of situation referred to here is one that tends to occur frequently between brothers and sisters. Although young children often seem to understand each other better than we understand them, there are many occasions when they do not. The situation is difficult enough for the child when an important adult will not accept his or her behaviour; but at least the adult can offer alternatives, distractions or limits that provide a sense of security. Seldom, though, would we hear one child say to another, 'Have this toy instead,' or 'Have I told you what I saw today?' or 'I'm not going to let you do that.' No wonder there is sometimes so much tension between children.

Children learn – often painfully – that other people don't automatically understand how they feel and what they want. It is part of the egocentric perspective not only to be oblivious of another's point of view, but also to assume that the other person is wholly conscious of yours. Mothers often manage to live up to this assumption to a remarkable degree in the first months and years; but in the process of widening their range of important people, it must come as a shock to many young children to find that this is very far from reality. No wonder they tend to struggle against the painful and bewildering realisation that the whole world, including their mother, does not revolve around them after all! Some children learn this reality quite quickly, especially those with brothers and sisters and confident parents; however, some may need special understanding and support when they come to playgroup, nursery or school.

Although it can be painful to find that other people matter too, this realisation makes life much more comprehensible for children. Learning to think about other people as well as themselves opens up the possibility that those people think about *them*, as well as themselves and other things. Once they understand that there *is* a reason for their important adults' 'unreasonable' behaviour, they in turn can 'deplore the behaviour', but not necessarily feel personally rejected.

– JOE'S TIGHT PLACE –

❛ *Lily's getting quite smart at knowing what's the matter with Joe, and how he feels. Not that she does much about it yet, though! But he seems to feel safe with her and maybe that's the reason.*

I had to stay home the other day so I was there all morning. Mum really knows what they like to play with; she came downstairs with Lily's dolls and a little pillow and the cover from the cot, and she just left them on the floor where Lily could find them. Lily couldn't wait to finish her drink; she put the pillow down on the floor near me and put the two dollies on the pillow. Joe was watching from his high-chair banging his biscuit on the tray and looking very sticky with his breakfast everywhere. Mum wanted me to change his nappy so we went upstairs. When I came back, Lily had got her dolls all tucked up under the cot cover really tight.

I sat down on the floor with Joe, and Lily came and sat beside me, but only for a minute; then she went and got her dolls and put them in a row next to us. I put Joe down at the end of the row too, and Mum said, 'One, two, three, four, five children in a row!' Lily looked really pleased; she likes things in their right places.

Joe didn't like it, though. He started crying and wanting to go back to Mum, and Lily looked resigned and furious all at the same time. She went over and sorted out the little pillow and cover again. She really wanted Joe to go to sleep on the doll's pillow; Mum didn't think it was a good idea, but Lily was so urgent about it that Mum gave in and put him down. He was quite happy for a bit, but then Lily tucked the cover around him very tight and rather near his face, and he cried. Lily held on to Joe really tight so Mum couldn't take him away but at the same time she looked up at us and said, 'Joe's worried', in a really understanding voice. She knew he didn't like it, but she wasn't going to let him go. The funny thing was, Joe didn't cry quite so loudly when she said that. **>**

> ## It is possible to accept and sympathise with babies' and young children's pain, anxiety and anger without having to accept 'unreasonable' behaviour generated by those feelings

Children's tolerance

One very positive aspect of young children is their ability to be tolerant and forgiving, especially with each other. This is often evident between children at nursery or playgroup, where they are making new friends and finding out how to get on with other people outside their family. For some children, this is a slow and difficult process, with much hurt and disagreement involved. Occasionally, others may stereotype such children as 'naughty' or 'rough', but it is astonishing how willing most children are to suspend judgement, and to accept, tolerate and support other children with difficulties, provided they have adult examples to follow, and support.

Sometimes things can be really hard for children on the receiving end of other children's anxiety or aggression, as well as hard, of course, for the one who is feeling anxious or angry. Unfortunately, because we would so much like to control or get rid of pain, anxiety and anger, our adult message is often, 'You're not really hurt', or 'There's no need to be frightened', or 'Don't be angry'. In other words, what we are saying is, 'Don't feel like that'.

If we can manage to allow children to keep their feelings, while at the same time being firm about what they are allowed to do, that helps them to be more accepting, but firm, both with themselves and with their more challenging friends.

Why say 'no' to smacking?

Unfortunately there is still considerable disagreement in the UK about the smacking of children, and despite an enormous amount of debate and lobbying a complete ban has yet to be achieved. Many people argue strongly that smacking is a violation of children's rights, and should be banned. Others say that smacking children teaches them the difference between right and wrong, and helps them grow up into responsible citizens. Others occasionally smack their children out of anger or irritation. Frank and open discussions about smacking usually generate a lot of feeling, and it is worth bearing in mind that people's views are likely to be influenced at least in part by their own experiences as children.

Smacking children is as much an assault as smacking adults (how puzzling that one is illegal, the other not) and especially with very young children the physical results can be grievous. From the perspective of this book – self-esteem and early learning – smacking as a means of discipline, or indeed for any reason, can be seen to be enormously counter-productive. In the same way that children learn to respect the feelings of others by having their own feelings respected, they learn much about how to express disagreement by experiencing how others do it. So in addition to the 'rights' and 'wrongs', it is worth considering the things we want our children to learn as they grow up, and what children actually do learn when they are smacked.

It is an inescapable fact that children learn indiscriminately from our example. This means that if parents – the people they most love and admire – use smacking as a way of saying 'no', children will be learning to say 'no' that way too. Most parents and teachers – and indeed governments – are anxious about the increase in crime and violence generally, and the way in which this affects their lives and the lives of their children. Consequently, their hopes for their children include learning to behave well and developing into responsible, law-abiding citizens. Most parents want their children to grow up knowing the difference between right and wrong. But what we *do* is much more powerful than what we *say*; and children tend to think that if hitting is all right for their parents to do, then it must be all right for them.

It is argued that smacking can be a very effective short-cut to achieving acceptable behaviour. The message to the child is clear and brief, and it is said that some children even seem to find a sense of relief in its use, as if it was actually needed. In fact, what *is* sometimes needed is a clear, firm message that means 'No'. Smacking is only one way to give this message – sometimes the easiest and most immediately effective way. The real price for giving what is in fact a very mixed message, comes later.

Children who are smacked are learning that when they *really* mind about something and they are not getting their way, in those circumstances it is all right to hit out. And if smacking has been the answer to the slightest irritation, then when children themselves get slightly cross they will behave in the same way. Many children are thoroughly confused. They may have been told to stand up for themselves physically, by parents who have never learned to be assertive in any alternative way themselves; but then they may have found themselves in trouble (even being smacked!) for hurting others, even though this is how they are treated themselves. Those who go along with the use of physical punishment should not be surprised or critical when children do the same; and they should be prepared for the fact that throughout those children's lives, the use of violence is liable to be – at least on first impulse – what they will do.

It is important to bear in mind that there are enormous temperamental differences in children which are evident in the ways in which they perceive how we treat them. One child might experience a push as disturbingly violent, whereas another would be oblivious to it. It is, of course, not the case that all children who go through a patch of hurting others are being smacked themselves. It may be, however, that a child who begins to hurt others is struggling with something which does, to him or her, *feel* like violence.

However, there seems to be increasing awareness of the importance for children to experience consistent limits and boundaries, enabling them to develop their own lasting self-discipline. What are the alternatives to smacking? First of all, parents do need to be clear with children that it is *never* acceptable to hurt another person on purpose'. Teaching young children *by example* how to say 'No' without smacking is also vital, so that children themselves can learn to be assertive, in non-violent ways. There are some suggestions about this in Chapter 6.

Here is Penelope Leach, in *Your Baby and Child* (2003, p. 473):

> *If children are neither to bully nor be bullied, they need to learn assertiveness, learn to express their own needs and feelings and defend their own rights, while respecting the rights and feelings of others.*

And if a parent does unintentionally smack (probably because of feeling under pressure in a difficult situation) it is best to try and find a way honestly to explain what happened, such as: 'I'm sorry I hurt you. I didn't mean to, but you made me so hurt/worried/cross'.

Much has been said in this book about children's need for acceptance – about acceptance (of feelings), and the child's corresponding need for limits (on behaviour). Miller (1992b, pp. 32–3) writes:

Four-year-olds need people who make limits clear, who just won't allow them to behave in an extreme way and who don't see them as too powerful . . . boundaries must be drawn, or any child grows anxious. . . . Limits are necessary in all sorts of ways, and the successful setting of them is a relief to a child.

Children need a structure within which to explore their world; they need people who are willing to say 'No' as well as 'Yes' calmly and consistently, so that they can feel respected and safe enough to get on with learning. Setting limits successfully is not easy, but in this increasingly violent world we urgently need to find non-violent ways of saying 'No' – ways that young children can both experience and practise. This would be a very individual but important contribution that every adult who lives or works with young children can make towards a less violent future.

– SHOPPING WITH DAD –

❛ *'Into the car everyone!' said the children's dad, 'We're going shopping.' Mum was out, and there was nothing for tea in the cupboard – not even chocolate biscuits! When we got to the shop, it was really quiet – everyone was watching the Grand National, Dad said. Lily rushed to get a trolley and Joe shouted and struggled to go in it. It was a long time since I had been shopping with them. There always used to be a fuss between them about riding in the trolley, but this time there wasn't, because Lily didn't want to anyway. She was too busy being grown-up and fetching things.*

Their dad didn't know where to find things nearly as well as Lily did; at least, he pretended he didn't. Lily was really good at knowing where to look and at getting the right make and the right amount. The trolley got quite full up, what with the things for tea and some toilet paper and nappies and Joe as well. 'A logical collection,' their dad said. 'Tea an' toilet paper an' Joe – make a good ad for nappies, wouldn't it?' Lily laughed as well when I laughed, although she didn't get the joke; but it made her feel even more grown-up to be laughing all together. And Joe jigged up and down, and waved and shrieked – he loves being in the trolley because he's nearer the conversation!

Then we had a bit of a disaster. Lily was supposed to be looking for toothpaste and she was gone quite a long time. We'd got in the queue by then, but we were just going to look for her when she came round the corner, looking solemn. You could see something was up, just by looking at her. She took her dad's hand and dragged him off, saying, 'Had 'n accident' in her grown-up, very deep voice.

I stayed with Joe, and when they came back they both looked pretty serious. Dad said she had tried to climb up the shelves to reach 'the pink toothpaste', but all the toothpaste and plastic shampoo bottles had crashed into a heap on the floor. It had taken them a long time to put them all back.

'Can't think why we didn't hear the crash,' said Dad to Lily, when at last we were in

the car. 'Sorry I wasn't there to catch you. That's what happens when you go climbing up shelves – lucky you didn't hurt yourself, wasn't it? But you remembered the chocolate biscuits!'

Then he turned round and grinned at her and she grinned back. **"**

Children learn to be responsible by taking responsibility

Using mistakes

Allowing responsibility is a tricky business. At the heart of the process is the question of whether the growing child will continue to *want* to take responsibility. Will the experience be sufficiently satisfying for the child to want to repeat it?

Our first and most important responsibility, as children and as adults, is for ourselves. We need to be able to be responsible for ourselves before we can take responsibility for other people and things. The more practice we have, the better we get at it. But we have to be careful about certain things if we want to be sure that our 'important children' continue to want to take responsibility – for themselves initially, and then in a wider sense for things, people and events in a variety of ways.

One of the most important things to be careful about is the need to keep the possibility of mistakes within safe boundaries. This means finding a balance between no possibility of a mistake (in which case the child may make no progress at all in learning to take responsibility) and the possibility of a very serious mistake (which might result in a determination not to risk anything so devastating again).

When things do go wrong, it is important that children feel safe to own up. This is not a moral issue, but a practical one about making sure that children do not give up the struggle of learning to do things for themselves, and for other people in a responsible way. It is absolutely crucial that children can risk making mistakes without fear of rejection. Genuine mistakes are, after all, only efforts gone wrong; nobody makes them on purpose. Children need to know that they will still be acceptable if they take responsibility for mistakes. Again, it is a matter of separating the child from the deed. If mistakes lead to disapproval and rejection, children will learn to avoid them, for disapproval and rejection are painful. But no mistakes means no exploring or trying anything unless children are sure they will get it right; and that rules out a lot of life and learning.

Some children learn not to admit disasters because they have found out that owning up is not safe – it hurts. The reason it hurts is because when someone rejects them, it makes them feel bad about themselves; this is the 'mirroring' process at work. After a while, a short-cut begins to occur whereby children feel bad about themselves when they make a mistake, even without any adverse comment from anyone else.

This is the start of a really slippery slope, the next step of which is not even to admit to themselves that something has gone wrong; they do this in order to avoid feeling even worse inside. Children – and adults – who really seem unable to admit even to themselves that they have made a mistake can be very difficult to get along with; but it is worth remembering that these people are hiding not only the mistake, but also a great deal of fear and pain. So allowing responsibility is indeed a tricky business unless we are prepared for children to make *manageable* mistakes and take responsibility for them, without fear of rejection.

Of course, it is important to be honest with children about the reality and significance of a mistake. They need to understand what has happened and why in order to learn from the experience. Some children make the same mistakes over and over again, and we sometimes attribute this to carelessness. But no one *wants* to go on making the same mistakes (unless it gives them satisfaction, in which case it's not a genuine mistake). These are the children who need help with recognising what is happening and why.

Learning from manageable mistakes is one of the most effective ways of learning, but it does need an element of reflection. This is something with which children may need adult help; some suggestions are made in Chapter 6.

Genuine praise

Another important factor in motivating children to take responsibility, is *genuine* recognition of their efforts and achievements. It really matters that we only give credit where it's due, and don't fall into the habit of praising on all occasions, 'to be on the safe side'. In fact, the safe side is just what it is not, as children who are praised indiscriminately soon come to suspect that all praise is meaningless. Instead of helping children to develop high self-esteem, this indiscriminate approach may have the opposite effect: it often fails to carry conviction at the time, and also prevents children from developing an 'inner yardstick' with which to evaluate their own efforts and achievements. Erikson (1950, p. 212) writes:

> In this [the development of self-esteem] children cannot be fooled by empty praise and condescending encouragement. They may have to accept artificial bolstering of their self-esteem in lieu of something better, but their ego-identity gains real strength only from wholehearted and consistent recognition of real accomplishment, i.e. of achievement that has real meaning in the culture.

Things are different then, for those children whose best efforts and achievements are consistently recognised. This is the way in which their positive self-concept develops, and it is positive self-concept which ultimately gives children that inner balance and confidence in their own ability which they need in order to make the very most of life.

Clearly, it is crucial that children feel safe to make 'manageable' mistakes and to 'own up' if they are to develop the ability to take responsibility for themselves and for other people and things. That their important people *realistically* recognise and value their efforts and achievements is also vital for their successful learning. Positive self-concept depends on recognising and valuing real effort and achievement.

6

Adults setting limits

– JOE'S CHANGED! –

❝ *When I came back from my holiday, Joe gave me such a surprise. He was bigger but it wasn't just that; he was more grown-up. At first I thought the biggest change was that he'd learned to crawl really fast; it meant he got around all over the place, instead of sitting there fretting. Mum and I knew if we didn't watch out, he'd hurt himself soon, particularly once he'd found out about climbing up on things, as well. He knows just what he wants and goes straight for it without stopping for anything – he goes so fast, too!*

When it came to tea-time that first day back, I could see there was another change as well. He'd got strong enough to be determined about things; not just about things he wants, but about things he doesn't want. I only noticed it when Mum went out suddenly because she'd forgotten to fetch something from the shop. She'd been in the middle of feeding Joe, one of his favourite green mushes she makes with left-over fish and peas. She pops another spoonful into his mouth as soon as he's swallowed the last one, and the first few mouthfuls go down really fast. But pretty soon he starts wanting to have the spoon himself and wanting to do it his way and then it goes all over the place – all over the table, on the floor – even in his hair! It reminded me of when Mum was feeding him herself and he used to take great gulps for the first bit and then start fooling around and wanting her to play.

Anyway they'd just got to the messy stage when she suddenly remembered about the shop, so she asked their dad to finish off with Joe; and then she was gone. That was when Joe got determined; he'd definitely had enough green mush, and then when his dad tried yoghurt, he only wanted two mouthfuls of that. What Joe wanted more than anything was to hold the spoon and do it himself, but his dad wanted him to eat some more without spreading it all around, so he kept trying. He gave Joe another spoon just to play with, but Joe still spat and dribbled and shouted and fussed; he wanted to do it all himself

In the end, his dad gave up. He said he wished Joe would eat his tea properly for once; he'd only be wanting it all over again in an hour or so. When Mum came back, Joe cried at her in a cross sort of way. It sounded like he was complaining about his

dad not understanding that he'd had enough to eat and wanted to play.
And their dad had to read the paper twice as long as usual, to recover! **"**

'Unreasonable' behaviour is almost always reasonable from the point of view of the baby or young child doing it

Two points of view

It could be said that it's all very well looking at the situation from the child's point of view, but what about our side of the picture? We're the adults. We know best.

It's helpful in this situation to remember that we don't have to give up our side of things, just because we've stopped to think about the child's side. What is important, though, is to let the child know that we *are* trying to understand. A change of perception on our part may well help us to be wiser in dealing with situations, but we may lose much of that advantage if we don't let children know about our efforts to understand them. The knowledge of our attention helps to give them a sense of security – or containment. That makes it easier for them to accept the adjustments we are asking them to make because of *our* point of view.

We may often ask ourselves why a child is behaving in a certain way and find that we have no idea of the answer. The inclination then, especially if this happens often, may be to give up trying to find the reason; it seems such a hopeless task. The thought that the child needs our acceptance anyway makes us all the more likely to grit our teeth and shrug our shoulders.

But there *is* a reason. Even though, if we knew what it was, it might seem extraordinary to us, nevertheless it would make sense to the child (although young children often do not have the words to explain the reasons for their feelings or their actions). Often, they don't really know what the trouble is themselves, or maybe they're too upset to explain it. Perhaps there has been a small (but important to the child) change in routine, or maybe something frightening has happened but no one else has noticed. In playgroup or nursery, perhaps they don't know the adult well enough to talk about it. When this happens, we can only do the best we can for the time being, which is to assume that the fuss is about something that matters, even though we don't know what. We still don't have to give in – often we *can't* give in – but we can sympathise.

Reflective talking about problems

Children often encounter difficulties that blow over almost immediately, and it's best simply to let things take their course. Sometimes, though, we know that something more serious is afoot. Maybe a child's behaviour noticeably alters, with more tears, quarrels or clinging than usual. Perhaps the sleep pattern is upset, or bed-wetting happens a lot. We tend to try and talk about these things when they occur, but those are the very times when the child may be least able to help by telling us what the matter is. When a child is clutching us frantically around the knees or crying passionately as soon as we appear after an absence, he or she is in no state to say anything that is likely to make sense.

This is when it may help to think about when there *will* be a quiet time to talk. Young children – like the rest of us – do need regular times to think and talk about what has happened to them and how they feel about it. Choosing the right moment needs careful thought: certain times of the day which may be particularly suitable for some children – maybe meal-times, bath-time or 'last thing' – can be battle-grounds for others. In playgroup, nursery and school settings, a special time during the session for discussing events and feelings can be very valuable.

Once the passion has blown over, a child may respond to a gentle question, especially if we adults can be quite calm and relaxed about it. For instance, 'You remember when you didn't want me to go this morning? When you cried? Can you remember what the trouble was?'

Sometimes the answer is quite straightforward, but occasionally the reason is too complex for a straight answer, and children may invent reasons that they think we will understand. It is as well to be prepared for this possibility; after all, we tend to do the same thing ourselves to them!

Talking about things calmly after the event can work well as a way of unscrambling quarrels, too. An example might be, 'Do you remember when you hit Joe this morning? He must have made you very cross – what was the trouble?'

This sort of conversation gives us a chance to suggest ways of dealing with pain, anxiety and anger so that they do not escalate.

Probably most of us would say that we long for the day when our children will understand and accept that they do have to do certain things. Of course, children have trouble with different things in different places, and while some seem to be born with the ability to take life as it comes, others seem to be ready to struggle all the way (Reid, 1992, p. 12). Frequent difficult areas include eating, sleeping, getting dressed, sharing, waiting, listening, keeping still, being quiet, as well as a great many other things that we want children to do! These things can be extraordinarily frustrating for them.

As adults, we have more or less learned that managing these things is essential, at least for most of the time, if we are to be acceptable to the people with whom we live. But young children don't know this. Until they begin to get the idea of taking responsibility for themselves, and until they begin to see things from another person's point of view, none of it makes much sense, and our insistence on these things is often very hard for them. It may help if we try not to ask for too much too soon and if we show that we want to understand what it feels like for them.

Being role models

Although our understanding often makes no difference to the outcome for the child, our attention to the causes of upsets is an important experience for children. Quite apart from the comfort of the moment, they are being shown a way of responding to other people that they may then learn to use for themselves. Then, when they are presented with *our* inexplicable demands, they may 'catch' the idea that there must be a reason, even if they can't understand it.

If this is true, then maybe we can show them something else, too, about looking for solutions. If *we* look for ways to compromise and to solve their problems, children may learn to look for solutions and accept compromises, too. This doesn't have to be a bargaining situation; perhaps more a case of us leading the way, with enough faith in children to know they will follow – in the end!

– EATING CUSTARD CREAMS –

❛ *I love watching Lily eating custard creams. I used to eat them like that, too. She takes the two halves apart, then she licks the cream off the insides and then she eats the boring outside bits – sometimes!*

This morning Lily had a dreadful cough, and Mum gave her a drink. After that, she opened a packet of Jammy Dodgers – they've got custard cream and jam in them as well – to cheer Lily up after all that coughing. Of course, when Lily had eaten the first one she wanted another; but Mum said if she really wanted another biscuit, she could have one of the other ones in the tin, but not another Jammy Dodger.

'I want a cream one.'

Mum said, 'No more Jammy Dodgers' again.

'But I want to choose,' said Lily getting furious.

Mum quietly said yes, she could choose between a malted one and a Rich Tea one out of the tin.

Lily was nearly into one of her screaming fits, but I could see there was a bit of her that quite liked Mum being firm; it made her feel safe to have Mum saying 'No' calmly, even though it made her want to scream as well. Just then Mum remembered that the cats hadn't had their breakfast. Lily loves helping to feed the cats, so she forgot all about biscuits and rushed to find the cat food.

Later on, Mum and Lily had another argument, this time about the telly. Lily just loves that programme about the puppets on the boat, and she went and switched on the telly much too early and sat right up close to it watching a really boring programme about selling cars. Mum turned it off, saying Lily had watched the telly too much yesterday morning, and she didn't really want to watch the boring programme about cars, and anyway Dan was coming to play soon.

'But we haven't seen this and we want to, don't we?' Lily said, looking at me. Mum glanced at me rather crossly, and said, 'Oh no you don't, do you?'

Meanwhile, Lily had turned the telly on again. Mum said she'd be really angry if Lily didn't stop. Instead of turning it off, Lily got out her Thomas the Tank Engine video and said, 'Well, we do want Thomas the Tank.' She looked at me determinedly. Mum heaved a sigh.

'I'll tell you what,' she said. 'You put in Thomas the Tank and get it ready but you're not to press the play button until Dan gets here. OK?'

So Lily got it ready; then she found her whistle in the bottom of the big dish in the kitchen and blew it really suddenly and loudly so we all jumped! ❯

It is possible to accept and sympathise with babies' and young children's pain, anxiety and anger without having to accept 'unreasonable' behaviour generated by those feelings

The need for limits

Adults living and working with children need to be able to offer acceptance and set limits, both at the same time. Children need security – both physical and psychological – to learn well, and this double security can only be achieved if we are consistent about the limits as well as the acceptance. An overdose of limits can eliminate confusion in the short term, but children then find it hard to take responsibility for themselves as they grow older.

On the other hand, real acceptance without any limits is frightening for children, and confusing too. Young children need to be clear about what is allowed and what is not; they need 'important people' who will not allow them to become too powerful or to behave in an extreme way (Miller, 1992b, pp. 28–33).

Developing self-discipline

One of our aims for children is likely to be that, ultimately, they grow out of the need for external limits and learn to regulate their own behaviour. This is another reason why acceptance and understanding are an important part of the picture. Children who have not been encouraged to think about how to behave in relation to what they want to do may well be good at doing as they are told; but sooner or later comes the time when they must think for themselves. Unexpected situations arise – more frequently as children grow older – when the rules don't seem to fit and there is no one to ask.

We cannot be there every minute of the day for ever. Children need to be developing an inner core of common sense upon which they can begin to rely. An important part of this common sense is their internalisation of their important people. In effect the child learns to think, 'What would mum/dad/my teacher have said?' So if we only say 'yes' or 'no', and if we don't do much honest explaining, we may leave children with very little to fall back on for themselves. They may be in a situation where, with no internal limits of their own, they must look elsewhere for rules. In adolescence there will be no shortage of alternatives, either: peer-group pressures and role models from videos and the television are two particularly powerful possibilities.

Establishing our priorities

If we want children to keep their balance in the face of these pressures, we must get in first, in early childhood; we must be willing to explain and discuss how we feel and why we do things. It helps to be clear, both to ourselves and to our children, about our priorities. Of course, it's really important that, for example, children know they must not run into the road without looking, and most children of four will say that hurting someone is wrong, although they may not know why. But finding out about what is allowed and what is not can be a confusing business for young children. Apparently it's fine to get in a mess making mud pies at playgroup in the morning, but not in the garden at home in the afternoon just before Gran arrives. It seems to be clever to make squiggly patterns with crayons all over the clean new book that Gran brings, but it's not all right to do it all over the not-so-new wallpaper in the bedroom. It's grown-up to mix flour and sugar and things when Mum's there to tell you how, but it's naughty to do it on your own.

We have a lot of listening and a lot of explaining to do. It helps children when we make a distinction between those things that *really* matter to us – like not running into the road and not seriously hurting people – and those things that are not of absolute importance yet, although we hope they will come to understand these soon. Whether they are at home or out, children need to know clearly which the important rules are.

When everything seems to be going wrong, it may be over-optimistic to try and put it all right at once. When it feels as though there's only one word in the language – 'no' – we can be sure that we are asking too much. No one can change everything they do all at once, especially not a young child; but maybe they can change one thing. Perhaps other things will right themselves, and if not, we can always tackle them later. The important question is, which thing should we concentrate on? When so many things seem to need sorting out, where is it best to start?

It can be helpful to talk this over with another adult; we sometimes get a better picture of what is happening that way. It helps to choose one thing that can solve other problems, too. For instance, if we are firm about putting the reluctant toddler to bed at a regular time and with a regular routine, that may be good news for older children who are needing their own time with us too, especially since the toddler was born.

Being consistent

It's hard enough for children to learn what is allowed and what is not in the normal course of events. We sometimes make it even harder for them by failing to be consistent about the rules. If children know that they're not allowed to eat in the front room, except when they can get away with it because mum and dad are too busy or tired to notice, then they never quite know whether today is one of those days or not; and if they are given an extra cuddle on Tuesday and sent to their bedroom on Wednesday, both because of arguments about sharing toys, what can they make of that? It would be unrealistic to expect that we can *always* be consistent in our reactions, but the more consistent we can manage to be, the more likely children are to be clear about what is allowed and what is not.

Another important aspect of consistency is that sooner or later children are going to discover about different values and priorities, even among their 'important people'; they are then faced with choices, uncertainty and opportunities to manipulate. We may be splendidly consistent as individuals, only to find that considerable confusion is caused by our failure to agree a common view with the child's other 'important adults'. It can be particularly helpful for staff in playgroups, nurseries and schools to bear this point in mind; children are likely to feel more secure where staff work as closely as possible with families so that similarities and differences can be identified and, if possible, discussed.

Sometimes, though, no amount of discussion achieves common ground, and the only course of action open to a child's 'important people' seems to be to agree to differ. When this happens, one way for everyone to help the child is to be open about the differences. For instance, 'I know Dad doesn't mind you bringing your bike in here, but I do, so please will you take it out again now?' or 'Mum wants you to stand up for yourself, doesn't she? So do I, but the way we do it at school is by talking, not hitting. . . . Have you tried saying, "No, don't do that"?'

Another form of inconsistency that is less straightforward is the one about treating individual children differently. Children are generally very quick to let us know when we are doing this, but they do need to learn that individual children, at different stages of their lives, need different rules. It is possible to be fair without treating children identically; indeed, it can be argued (and often is, by older children) that to accord the same privileges at the same time is most unfair.

Behind the child's 'It's not *fair*' is really the cry 'You don't love *me* as much'. Surely no 'important person' in the world is immune from this cry and from the guilt it generates. Privileges and presents do not solve it, though; in fact, they may even confirm the child's suspicion that we have something to feel guilty about. If there is an answer, it lies in 'unconditional acceptance' (described in Chapter 1) and the combination of efforts to understand our important children, together with calm, firm setting of limits.

Temper tantrums

Temper tantrums are extremely common in very small children. It is estimated that nearly 20 per cent of two- and three-year-olds have a tantrum at least once a day, with a much higher proportion having the occasional tantrum (Goldschmied and Jackson, 2004, p. 220). As very small children have such a high level of frustration, together with such a limited command of language, this is not at all surprising. Goldschmied and Jackson's advice, (2004, p. 220) is particularly helpful:

> *At moments like this, it is clear that words are quite useless, in fact any attempts to check the tantrum generally make things worse.*
> *The most helpful thing for the adult to do is to stay near the child, perhaps sitting down, attentive and available but not intervening until the child is quiet again. It is often noticeable that other children watch very carefully and are reassured that [the adult] stays calm and, once the tantrum has passed, helps the child; with a drink of water and quiet words, to feel all right again.*

Goldschmied and Jackson also mention that some children who have frequent tantrums may have learned that this is the best (or only) way to get what they want, and that we should try to avoid reinforcing this behaviour. Although sometimes tantrums seem to occur without any warning, quite often we can see them looming all too easily. Brazelton (1992) proposes talking about an issue with the child before things go too far: presenting choices and explaining the way we would like the child to behave. He suggests that, if we definitely want a child to do something, we should never ask, 'Will you?' but instead should say 'Now it's time.' Penelope Leach's thoughtful section on tantrums (2003, pp. 376–9) reflects her wisdom and experience and repays careful reading.

Television, videos and DVDs

The impact of television, videos and DVDs on young children is enormously important. The results of television viewing can have a major effect on their development, their consciousness and their learning (Singer and Singer, 1990, pp. 176–98). Although it can be argued that there are benefits for children in watching television, it may be appropriate to set some limits about what children watch and for how long. The increase of television sets in children's bedrooms is deeply worrying.

In households where the television remains on throughout the day, babies have difficulty in learning to distinguish their mother's voice from other voices. Turning the TV off sometimes, even if only for half an hour, can make a difference provided someone spends that time talking and playing with the baby.

The debate about the impact of television needs to be seriously discussed in all those places where children live their lives. We need to gain information, discuss appropriate responses and act. Meanwhile, it is a good idea to join children in their viewing as much as possible. This way, we can help children to begin to develop the important ability to look critically at programmes and films, and learn to discuss them. Then, rather than the possibility of an isolating, frightening or confusing experience, watching can become a social event.

– DAN STAYS THE NIGHT –

❝ *Lily's friend Dan came to sleep last week. His mum and dad were going to see his gran, and his mum thought he'd be better with us. It was the first time he'd slept the night away from home, and Lily and Dan had such a good time that now Lily wants to go and sleep with him; Mum says maybe, one day.*

Dan arrived at bath-time, so they scampered off upstairs. You should have seen the bathroom after that! Mum said Dan's the bravest bath-swimmer she's ever seen. Lily has just learned to put on her own pyjamas, and she promised to help Dan if he was good, and no grown-ups were allowed. When they came out of the bedroom, it was hard not to laugh because they looked so solemn and funny; Lily's pyjamas were inside out, and Dan's bottoms were on upside-down. They were pleased to have managed on their own, but I think they guessed that things weren't quite right. Mum says we mustn't laugh when Lily makes funny mistakes, otherwise she'll stop trying, so we managed to be serious and say how clever they were to manage to get them on.

Mum let them lay the table for tea, too. They were so proud of themselves when they'd done it all. Dan even remembered the salt and pepper. Lily said 'What about flowers?' and that was where the trouble started.

Mum gave Dan a little pot and said they could pick three flowers each out of the back garden. Lily liked that, because she knows how many three is. They rushed off together and a minute later we heard a crash.

'Oh no,' groaned Mum. 'I knew I shouldn't have given them that one.'

Outside, Lily was looking at the smashed pot, and Dan was nowhere to be seen.

'Dan dropped it,' Lily said. 'Can we have another one?'

'Where's Dan?' asked Mum.

'I don't know,' said Lily. 'Behind the shed.'

They went down the garden to Lily's favourite hiding place behind the shed. Dan was there, looking a bit flushed.

'It was Lily,' he said.

'What was Lily?' asked Mum.

'Lily dropped it.'

'No, I didn't,' said Lily indignantly.

'It's all right, Dan,' said Mum, holding out her hand. 'Let's go and pick up the pieces.'

'I didn't do it. She did it,' he insisted.

'No, I didn't,' said Lily again hotly.

Mum looked at them thoughtfully.

'It's hard to say it's your fault if you think you're going to get into trouble,' she said to no one in particular. 'Let's not worry about who did it just now. Perhaps we'll talk about it later.' She walked back towards the house.

'Who's going to find three flowers for the table?' she asked over her shoulder.

When Lily's dad came back, he thought the table looked wonderful, especially the flowers in the egg-cup.

'We did it,' they shouted, jumping round him.

Tea-time is always special, because everyone's together and it's the best time to talk about things. Sometimes Joe fusses or makes an awful mess, but he's learning; he wants to be big like Lily, so he copies her. Dan wanted to get down and play because they don't have tea together in his house; but when Mum and Lily's dad started talking about having the builders last summer, he changed his mind. I think they did it on purpose – Dan always wants to talk about builders.

Then we talked about breaking things and having accidents and what upsets people. Lily said she hates it when people say she did something when she didn't. I don't know if she was thinking about Dan or if she had forgotten and was saying it anyway. Dan said he hates it when grown-ups are cross, and Mum said she might be sad if someone had an accident with something precious, but she wouldn't be cross. Then Dan said he had had an accident today when he dropped the pot, and Mum said it was really grown-up and brave of him to tell her about it. When she said that, Dan looked really pleased and happy

Dan and Lily didn't go to sleep until very late; I think they tried but it was too exciting. In the end, Mum got a bit cross with them because she was afraid they would wake up Joe. **❯**

Children learn to be responsible by taking responsibility

Encouraging independence

The first form of responsibility that means something to young children is the responsibility for looking after themselves. There are all sorts of ways in which we can encourage them to learn to be independent and to take responsibility for themselves, and the achievement of each small step, together with our recognition of it, gives them the satisfaction and motivation to tackle the next.

Some of the areas that tend to cause most tension in the early years – eating, sleeping, toileting, clothes and siblings – also contain particular opportunities for growing independence (see Chapter 5 for ways of using children's mistakes positively and giving genuine praise when appropriate). These are ways in which children can be supported and encouraged towards independence.

When children are having trouble with eating or sleeping, when they can't seem to get the hang of using the toilet, or when they seem to spend the whole day quarrelling with a brother or sister, they may need the safety of 'no blame' in these areas in order to make progress. We adults know what it feels like to get blame rather than sympathy for a mistake we never meant to make, and how readily we resolve never to risk *that* again! However, it's often hard for us not to blame young children when we so often find ourselves dealing with the consequences; and, of course, it's important to involve children in the consequences of their mistakes, too, in a positive and sensitive way. Our reward for resisting blaming them as well comes in the shape of children who will always be willing to 'have a go'.

Recognising real achievements

Families, playgroups, nurseries and schools need a culture of recognition and acceptance, not only of mistakes, but of successes too. This is something about which 'important adults' can lead the way, although it seems that many of us find it hard. We tend to be much more aware of our failures than our successes and often find it uncomfortable and rather embarrassing to own up to our achievements.

Our embarrassment can rub off on the children who live with us, in the same way that other attitudes do, but there is no need for this to happen, once we are aware of it. Realising our power as role models, we 'important adults' can help in families and other places where children live their lives, by being open about our own efforts and achievements, and by noticing and praising each other. It is worth making a habit of recognising, accepting and celebrating success, in ourselves, in each other and in our young children.

However, there is a pitfall to watch out for here. Curry and Johnson (1990, pp. 91–2) emphasise that making a habit of celebrating success only works if the successes are real; and that heavy doses of well-intentioned but often empty praise can be counter-productive. The need to praise children appropriately for genuine effort and real achievement means that we need to know a lot about levels of understanding and their skills. Only this way can we appreciate the extent of their efforts and achievements and recognise 'true accomplishments'.

Parents are the experts in relation to their own children and know by living with them day by day when they are making efforts and when they are achieving. Adults in early years settings will know about child development generally, but can usefully develop ways of working together with parents in order to know more about individual efforts and achievements (Whalley, 1994, p. 56). We need *accurate* knowledge about children, and this highlights the necessity for effective methods of observing, assessing and recording children's progress (Bartholomew and Bruce, 1993, pp. 1–6).

It may seem contradictory to find so many suggestions about success and praise in a chapter about setting limits; this, though, is the other side of the coin – the important *context* for success in calmly, firmly and consistently setting the limits young children need.

POSTSCRIPT TO PART 3: ABOUT OTHER PEOPLE

Living or working with young children?
Questions to think about . . .

> **'Unreasonable' behaviour is almost always reasonable from the point of view of the baby or young child doing it**

1. Think back to a time when a child was behaving 'unreasonably'. What might have been the reasons?

> **It is possible to accept and sympathise with babies' and young children's pain, anxiety and anger without having to accept 'unreasonable' behaviour generated by those feelings**

2. Are you aware of consistent patterns of 'unreasonable' behaviour? From a starting-point of acceptance and sympathy, is there anything to be done to avert them?

> **Children learn to be responsible by taking responsibility**

3. What are some of the practical ways in which very young children can be offered genuine responsibility?

RECOMMENDED FURTHER READING

For sharing with children . . .

Rathmann, P. (1994), *Good Night, Gorilla,* **London, Puffin Books**
Good Night, Gorilla is a great fantasy, full of humour and excitement. A blissfully unaware zoo-keeper is followed home to bed by a procession of animals helpfully released by the gorilla. Just as everyone is about to drop off Mrs Zoo-Keeper realises there is company in the bedroom and blearily returns them all to the zoo – almost! Children always laugh at this brilliant book.

Burningham, J. (1973), *Mr Gumpy's Outing,* **London, Puffin Books**
This picture book is a classic, for very good reasons. Mr Gumpy takes the children, the rabbit, the cat, the dog, the pig, the sheep, the chickens, the calf and the goat for a day out on the river. They fall in, climb out, and trek home across the fields for the sort of tea we all dream about. Dignified, lovable Mr Gumpy knows all about acceptance.

. . . and for a good read

Goldschmied, E. and Jackson, S. (2004) *People Under Three: Young Children in Day-Care,* **(Second Edition) London, Routledge**
For people working in day-care this book is a unique resource – all the more so because comparatively little has been written on day-care for under threes. The book is organised chronologically from babyhood to the end of the third year, covering all the things that matter most to young children in a way that is entirely helpful to practitioners. The combination of sound theory, practical common sense and wisdom with which babies and young children are understood makes compelling reading. If there were only one book to read about people under three in day-care, this would be it.

PART 4

LINKING WITH LEARNING

7

Children's ways of learning

– GOING TO NURSERY SCHOOL –

❝ The other day Mum got a letter from the nursery school. It said that after Christmas, Lily can go every day in the mornings, and would she and Mum like to come and visit sometimes? Mum said, 'What a good idea', but then she thought that, as Joe might be a nuisance and swallow things, perhaps I could take Lily instead of her. When she explained this to the school, they said it was quite all right about Joe, and they like having toddlers around. But Mum said she'd worry about Joe anyway so I'd better go for most of the visits. We all went the first time, though: Lily and Joe and Mum and me.

Lily had a great time. They had all her favourite things – painting and drawing and cutting and gluing – and lots of things to play with in the garden. She did a special painting for her dad. She said it was him in bed, and you could see where his head was, and she did Toby on the bed too. She said he was purring because her dad was cosy. Mum was just saying how lovely it was, when Lily started putting black paint all over the top of it. Mum said, 'Don't spoil it,' but Lily wouldn't stop. She said it was night-time and she was painting the dark!

There were two other children with their mums there as well, but they had done lots of visiting already. You would have thought that Lily was the old hand, though, and they were the new ones. Mum got talking to one of the other mums who said that her little boy Max hadn't played much with other children before they came to nursery. He spent all the time as near to his mum as he could get. The trouble was, his mum thought it would be best if she left Max to get on with it. I heard her say to the teacher that she thought it was time for her to go, but she knew he would make a fuss, so she was going to go without telling him. The minute she said that, the teacher stopped what she was doing and they had a talk about it.

The teacher said it would be a bad idea to go away without telling Max. She was very nice, but very definite about it. She asked if the mum had ever gone away without telling him before. The mum said she had, and that apparently he'd made a big fuss when he'd found she'd gone, but he'd stopped crying quite soon. She asked why it was a bad idea. The teacher said because then he'd never know when she might *disappear. It would make him worry and want to hang on to her all the more. She said children usually stopped crying after their mums or dads have gone because there's no point in crying then – it doesn't bring them back. It doesn't always mean they feel better, though. The teacher said that it would be best if the mum promised Max that she wouldn't go without telling him – then he could get on with playing without worrying.*

In the middle of this, Max suddenly came and grabbed his mum round the knees – he must have noticed her talking to the teacher and guessed they were talking about his mum going. The mum looked rather desperate and said how was she ever going to leave him then. The teacher said that if she promised not to go without telling him, then Max would feel safer with her still here and he would soon realise that it's safe without her as well. He would stop worrying enough to see that the teacher looks after children all right until their mums come back.

There was another mum who couldn't leave her child either. It was when Mum took Lily to find the toilets that I noticed them. The little girl was called Kimberley, and her mum helped her a lot. I heard Kimberley say she wanted to do a painting; if Lily had said that, Mum would have said things like 'OK' and 'Don't forget to put on an apron' and 'Can I see it when it's finished?' and maybe even 'Can I come and watch?' This mum hovered around sorting out the apron, choosing the colours and fussing about the paper: Then, when Kimberley said she wanted to go out, she had to just stand there while her mum changed her shoes and put on her coat for her. After all that, she wouldn't go out without her mum coming with her, so there was a long wait while her mum got dressed too.

I thought that Kimberley wouldn't ever learn how to do things herself because she didn't need to, with her mother doing them for her all the time. Perhaps the mum didn't really like the idea of Kimberley managing without her. If the mum thinks Kimberley won't be able to manage on her own, maybe Kimberley will think that too. Then she'll think she can't do things, instead of knowing she can.

Lily told her dad all about her new nursery at tea-time. She gave him the black painting and she had to tell him all about what was under the black paint because it was dark. Then she remembered some things at the nursery that Mum and I hadn't even noticed, like the milk they drink out of little bottles and the boy called Omar who played with her in the garden. There was a really big cardboard box, and they had both got inside and pretended it was their house.

When her dad asked, 'What are you going to do when you go next week?', she said, 'Pretend with Omar'. ❜

Learning involves struggle and adjustment. Too much struggle is overwhelming. Too little struggle means no adjustment

Children learning

Young children – and adults too – learn well with an appropriate level of challenge; this is more helpful than overwhelming demands on the one hand, or nothing with which to struggle on the other. Piaget's theoretical model of adaptation, in which he describes 'accommodation' and 'assimilation' (Piaget, 1953, pp. 407–19), suggests a model for the way in which learning takes place. The work of Athey has done much to illuminate our understanding of Piaget's thinking. She shows (1990, pp. 75–6) that the way in which we learn ranges from struggle and practice to play:

> . . . new knowledge is associated with struggle and well-assimilated knowledge is usu-
> ally accompanied by feelings of confidence (competence generates confidence). 'Play-
> fulness' signifies knowledge that is so well assimilated that it can be played with.

Elaborating on Chukovsky's idea (1966, pp. 96–8) that it is only when a child knows something very well that he or she can play with it, Athey gives the example of the game of 'Ring-a-ring o' roses'. When toddlers fall down, they are usually furious because falling down means failure to stand up, whereas slightly older children, who are having fun with pretend falling down, are signifying real competence in staying upright. Struggle indicates new knowledge, whereas playfulness indicates well-assimilated knowledge.

Bruce (1991, p. 34) uses the diagram below to illustrate the relationship of the terms 'accommodation' and 'assimilation'.

accommodation				assimilation
◄───►				
struggle	practice	play	humour	bored

Working together on the Froebel project (Athey, 1990, p. 76), Athey and Bruce recorded different kinds of children's responses in the project environment. They discovered that over 80 per cent of responses were accommodatory (surprise, per-turbation, struggle, absorbed or focused attention) and – unexpectedly – that only slightly more than 5 per cent of responses were assimilatory, showing playfulness and humour. A possible explanation for this was thought to be that the stimulating environment of the project generated struggle and other accommodatory responses.

However, as it is well-assimilated knowledge that stays in the mind and contin-ues to be of use, this finding raises questions about what constitutes the very best learning environment for young children. It is often suggested that what children need is plenty of stimulation; but, although stimulation is clearly important, per-haps we should not lose sight of the need for a balance. If we want long-term benefits from early childhood education, and if we value the development of imagination, creativity and originality in young children, it will be important to include in the learning environment many opportunities to play and be creative with those things with which children are already familiar.

In Lily's nursery, the boy called Max whose mother wanted to 'leave him to get on with it' was overwhelmed. He had little experience of playing with other children, and so had few ideas to 'hang on to' in the new situation. In addition to that, his previous experience of his mother leaving him had been too bewildering to be of use to him in the new situation. His mind could not accommodate the unthinkable possibility of being in the nursery with so many unknown children and adults, and without his mother. Lily, on the other hand, knew a lot already about how to make new friends, and had learned that Mum is both predictable and reliable about going away and coming back; she doesn't go without telling Lily and she comes back when she says she will. Because of this, Lily could manage the new situation by building on previous experience, whereas Max's experience was too limited or too negative to help him.

Kimberley, whose mother wanted to do things for her all the time, was also having difficulties. With few challenges, there was little opportunity for her to add to her existing knowledge and understanding. Nor did she have the opportunity to adjust her current knowledge and understanding in the light of new information. This is the reason for the early education principle that, with all new learning, it is essential to 'start with the child'. New ideas or experiences make sense to children if they can be 'attached' to previous relevant experience.

Manageable experiences

There needs to be some sort of challenge or tension for learning to take place. If nothing is new or challenging, then nothing changes and we make no progress. The mother in Lily's nursery who didn't let her child do things for herself was getting in the way of the child's learning. We tend to think that total absence of stress is the ideal state: no quarrels to resolve, no problems to overcome, no difficulties to face. Such a state may seem wholly desirable, but it is uncreative. It is a manageable level of struggle which constitutes the most exciting, satisfying and fruitful situations in terms of learning. A good early childhood education setting where children learn effectively will be physically, socially, emotionally and cognitively interesting and challenging.

If left to their own devices, children in play automatically regulate their own levels of challenge. On the one hand, too little challenge leads to boredom and a desire for something else to happen; we often describe bored children as 'looking for trouble', and indeed they are, in a sense, genuinely looking for problems to solve. On the other hand, too much challenge results, in a variety of ways, in a retreat to safer ground.

A safe environment

A few decades ago, this regulating function was much in evidence in children's play outside the home – in streets and parks and playgrounds. Their play with friends outside the home was a crucial source of learning. Now the only secure alternative to playing out, where children can genuinely explore their world in safety, is the good early childhood education setting where exploration is encouraged. For most children, the world outside the home and away from 'important adults' is not generally a safe place to play. The congestion on our roads and the dimension of 'stranger-danger' are such that the challenges children are liable to meet outside the home without an adult may well be more devastating than manageable. As 'important people', we may have to recognise that allowing children to 'play out' represents an unacceptable risk.

This is a serious situation in terms of children's learning: they are being deprived of one of the main ways of learning about themselves, each other and their world. Increasingly, doors and windows are closing on children's opportunities for safe, challenging play with other children. Neighbourhoods are not safe, and nursery education is not universally available to those children who need it. In recognising the consequences of this situation, we need to look carefully not only at what has been lost, but also at what is taking the place of this sort of play. It is profoundly worrying that, for many children, current alternatives may be limited to solitary play in the home and often to long hours in front of the television. These alternatives do not contain the learning experiences that children need for a rich childhood and for their normal development. It should surely be part of the social policy of national and local government to ensure that all children have the opportunities they need for safe play.

– PIPES AND GUTTERS –

❛ Now Lily's at nursery every morning, I don't see her so much; but the other day Mum said she thought they might like an extra pair of hands there sometimes, and would I like to go and help once a week? I think she really wants to go herself, but she can't just now, so I'm going instead. Sometimes there's lots to do, and I'm too busy to see what Lily's up too, but I can usually watch her for some of the time.

It was a lovely day last week when I went, and the best thing was the sandpit in the garden. They had lots of pipes and gutters in the sand; some of the children wanted a water-run, and they'd worked out with the teacher how you could fit the pipes together and balance the top bit on a tower of milk crates. They've got a tap on the wall near the sandpit where the children can fill up their buckets, and the water they fetched went down all the pipes and into the big bucket at the bottom. Lily had a great time standing on a milk-crate and pouring her bucket of water into the top bit. After she'd done it, she scrambled down as fast as she could and rushed to see if the water was *going into the bucket. Sometimes it fell out of a hole half-way down, and then she had to try and mend it. It always took a bit of thinking out, and sometimes it didn't work the first time and she had to try something else.*

Once she couldn't manage to make the corner bit stay on the pipe, and I thought she was going to make a big fuss, but the teacher helped her just in time. I thought the teacher was great, the way she knew exactly when Lily was nearly giving up. Then she just helped Lily enough so she could carry on.

When Lily tried to explain about the pipes and gutters to her dad, he said he didn't know what she meant, and couldn't she draw a picture to show him? She really wanted him to know about the pipes and she took ages drawing a plan of just how she remembered them. We all thought the plan was so good that she took it to show her teacher the next day; and the teacher thought it was so good that she put it up in a special place on the wall so everyone could see it. Lily felt really proud of herself then. **,**

Some learning skills come naturally; these include exploring, questioning, experimenting and learning from mistakes

---

Exploratory learning

Babies are seeking creatures. They watch and listen and touch and smell and taste, working away at finding out. They are struggling for knowledge and control. As they grow in competence, their need to explore and control becomes increasingly demanding for us adults. Our efforts to contain this need result in much frustration for all concerned. Of course, much of the exploring must be contained for safety's sake, but the outcome may be, at least partially, to limit the child's development.

Isaacs (1954, p. 9) referred to the way in which children actively explore in order to solve their problems:

> *We have only to watch this play with a discerning eye, and to listen to his comments and questions, in order to realise how his mind is beset with problems of one sort or another – problems of skill, problems of seeing and understanding, problems of feeling and behaviour . . . He is always, in his own mind, concerned with watching and trying to understand and to deal with things and people, the objects in the world outside him, which he so much needs to master and to comprehend.*

This consciousness of problems to be solved and the drive to tackle them is, Isaacs said, the key to children's mental development. It unlocks the meaning of their behaviour.

Lily's efforts in the sandpit with the pipes and gutters were about investigating and controlling those objects. She was trying out ways of doing what she wanted, discovering new strategies and discarding old ones. She talked to the teacher while she was doing it, asking questions and trying new ideas. This exploring of the pipes and asking questions of the nearest adult was normal and natural for her. Another child might have been more reticent, but reticence comes when children are suppressing their exploring instincts.

Most 'important people' have a general idea of how they want their children to be and what they want them to know. If little progress is made with these aims, we have a tendency to say that a child is not learning. It can be challenging, but also useful, to realise that young children are inevitably and continuously learning; they do not remain blank until they can take in what we want them to know, but, like sponges, they constantly absorb an amazing amount of knowledge and under-standing. They do not discriminate between what we want them to know and what we do not; they learn about all sorts of things that come their way. Smith (1978, p. 8) makes the point:

Children spend the first years of life solving problems all the time. Probably more learning takes place in the first two years than in any similar period thereafter. Children are born learning; if there is nothing to learn, they are bored, and their attention is distracted elsewhere. We do not have to train children to learn, or even account for their learning: we have to avoid interfering with it.

When a child does not seem to have learned what we hoped, instead of thinking that nothing was learned, it can be instructive to wonder what was learned instead. We may expect that a day in school will result in a greater understanding about, for instance, number concepts; yet the increase in understanding may be more related to problems of feeling and behaviour. An outing to the wildlife park will surely result in greater knowledge of the habits of monkeys, but the real lesson in life may turn out to be the use and misuse of public services, such as buses and lavatories. It may seem that a child has learned absolutely nothing from an experience such as an expedition to the supermarket; but much may actually have been learned or con-firmed about adult expectations of behaviour in public, and individual levels of tol-erance. It is not so much a question of whether children are learning, as what they are learning.

Children learn actively from their 'important people' and from the situations in which they find themselves. This is a challenging thought: what *are* they learning from living with us?

– BEING GOOD –

❝ There's a little girl in Lily's group called Aisha. She's interested in what the others are all doing and she spends lots of time watching them, but she can't seem to join in. She seems to be really stuck. At first, I thought it was just because she wasn't used to being *at nursery and maybe she felt a bit scared of doing anything in case she got it wrong. Some children seem to think everything's got to be right first time – they think there's only going to be one right way to do everything and they want you to tell them what it is. But then they don't have the fun of trying things out or the satisfaction of sorting something out for themselves.*

Aisha's mum really looks after her. When she brings her in the morning, she makes sure she's got everything she needs and she gives her a great big hug and tells her to be good. Aisha really wants to please her mum and the teacher. Maybe that's why she doesn't try things out, or ask about things. Maybe she thinks if you make a mistake or don't know about something, it's not being good.

Yesterday, the teacher had mixed up some stuff for the children to play with and it was really messy. She told me that the children always love the way it looks different from how it feels, and they learn a lot of early maths and science from playing with it. It's made of mixed-up cornflour and water and it looks all wet and sloppy but when you touch it, it feels dry. Lily thought it was wonderful – she spent ages scraping it up with her fingers and pouring it into little measuring pots and pretending things about it. All the time she was talking with the teacher about what she was doing, and so were the others. Aisha stood behind the teacher and watched. But she wouldn't join in, so she never found out what the messy stuff felt like and how it pours into other things – and she missed a lot of fun.

After a while, the teacher left those children to get on by themselves and went to help some other children cook some little carrot cakes; she said she'd better keep an eye on them because you have to do cooking right if you want to eat it. Aisha went too. I stayed to keep an eye on the cornflour, so I didn't see what happened next, but I heard the teacher telling Aisha's mum that Aisha had helped to make the cakes, so she must have felt all right about cooking. I wonder why she could do that, but not mess about with cornflour?

In order to be 'socially acceptable', children often learn to behave in ways that inhibit learning

Adult expectations

If they are to thrive, babies and young children need their 'important people's' acceptance. The way in which they learn to be acceptable has been described earlier: initially, the interaction between the mother and baby sets the scene, and this is developed further by other important people in the family, and gradually outside the family, too. Babies and young children learn which of their actions give particular pleasure, and lead to warm acceptance by their important people. Clearly, every important person will be unique in their values, but children learn that certain characteristics are particularly acceptable to parents and to teachers (Drummond, 1993, pp. 9–11).

Most children know that being acceptable generally involves obedience. When asked the question, 'When are your parents pleased with you?' (Roberts, 1993, p. 58), one child stated with clarity the principle that many others struggled in various ways to express. He said, 'You have to do what they say.' As soon as 'being good' was seen to be the issue, the discussion flowed. By the time they are three or four, children seem to be quite ready to identify what it means to be good. Although there may be disagreements between them about what is good and what is not, each child reckoned he or she had the answers; after all, they need to know. It is interesting that many of the answers seemed to be the result of *watching* what happens to others, rather than, for instance, remembering instructions. There seemed to be general agreement, among both children and adults, that being good means being obedient, especially when outside the home.

It requires considerable mental balance – which even many adults fail to attain – to be appropriately obedient *and* to ask questions. Is it realistic to expect children to do this? Does a four-year-old know when to conform and when to explore? Is it reasonable to expect young children to experiment and learn from mistakes at the same time as trying to be 'good'?

It may be that the situation is not as stark as this at home, but there can be little doubt that, outside the home, these are real questions for children, and therefore real questions for parents, teachers and others. To safeguard their perception of themselves as exploratory learners, they need their entitlement: enough freedom to explore their world.

8

Adults supporting learning

− TOO MUCH FOR TERRY −

❝ There was lots going on at the nursery when we went this week. I don't know how the teacher keeps an eye on it all. There were two students there a bit older than me, and they had to do something with the children and then write about it. I'd heard the teacher talking to them about it last week. She told them it wasn't enough to think about what the children needed to know and how they were going to teach them; they needed to watch the children more before they decided what to do. She said that if they chose something to do that wasn't connected with what the children know a bit about already the children wouldn't be able to make sense of it. The best way to find out what young children know about and what they're interested in, is to watch them and listen to them, she said.

I decided I would do a bit of watching and listening myself, when I wasn't doing things they asked me to do. It was a real eye-opener. There's a boy called Terry who never plays with the other children. When he first came to nursery his mum stayed with him for weeks and weeks because he didn't feel safe. Now he feels safe with his teacher and he even goes off and plays on his own sometimes, but not with the others. Anyway, yesterday I watched him.

He spent a long time sticking lots of those cardboard rolls that you get in the middle of cling film onto the top of a cereal box. He was really careful about it, and when he'd done about five in a row, he left the model on the bench − I don't know what it was supposed to be − and went off outside. Then Fatima came along and started cutting up bits of paper with what the children call the jiggy-jaggy scissors; they cut sort of teeth shapes. She said she was making a crocodile. Then she saw Terry's model on the table and she said, 'This can be my crocodile,' and she stuck the teeth onto the end of the box. There was an amazing collection of wood sticks and things in a box for making models with, and one of the mums asked Fatima why she didn't make her crocodile a cage? She said crocodiles are really dangerous, and we wouldn't want this one getting out, would we?

Fatima loved it. She was just putting the crocodile into the cage, when Terry came back. He watched her without saying anything. Then he saw me watching, and he came over and said, 'That's mine'. Fatima was so keen on her game with it that I asked

86

him if she could borrow it for a bit longer. I said she'd made it into a crocodile and that she'd give it back to him very soon. He looked at me gloomily, then he looked at her playing with his model and then he turned round and went back into the garden. At first I thought that meant it was OK, but it wasn't. It was only because I caught sight of his face as he went through the door that I realised he was just beginning to cry.

It took ages to sort it out. First of all, Terry was so upset that he could only cry and not talk about it. Then he said he didn't want his model to be a crocodile. I asked why he didn't say that before and I tried to say that he should tell people what he wants and doesn't want, but I don't think he was listening; it was all too much. I knew we'd have to get the crocodile back from Fatima and take its teeth off, and I thought there'd be even more of a fuss about that, from her. I said to her that Terry was really upset, that we'd have to give his model back and that she could start again and make one all for herself. But she didn't mind at all; she looked at him carefully and then she just said 'OK, he can have it,' quite cheerfully and went off to do something else.

The teacher says Terry didn't get a chance to play with other children of his age much before he came to nursery and that Fatima's got a twin brother, so she's had more practice. She says Terry's getting better all the time, though. Perhaps that's why he didn't stand up for himself and why Fatima could manage without a fuss.

The students had a disappointment. They only come once a week, so this was their special day. They'd noticed last week that the children were interested in painting and mixing colours, so they decided to see if the children would be interested in doing a big green picture with just blue and yellow paint. The trouble was, they forgot to check with the teacher, so they didn't know the children often do that sort of thing and had done a big picture about mixing colours only two days before. They'd got it all ready at college, so when they got to nursery it was too late to change. It was a pity because nobody wanted to do it. When I showed Lily what the students had got ready she said, 'Done it,' and went off to play with Omar. In the end, they found a little group of girls who always like making things, but even they didn't stay very long or want to talk about it much, because it was nothing new or different.

The teacher said they were quite right to choose something like that, really, but that it needed to have something slightly different and special about it, otherwise the children wouldn't learn anything. **'**

Learning involves struggle and adjustment. Too much struggle is overwhelming. Too little struggle means no adjustment

Levels of challenge

Children learn in situations which are neither undemanding nor overwhelming. We can use what we know about the process of learning to help children to build on what they already know, giving them opportunities to struggle, practise and play. This works best when we can incorporate security and enthusiasm into the child's learning. To do this, we need to know not only how to help them feel safe, but also about their previous knowledge, their particular interests and their individual patterns of learning.

It is a process of matching children's existing knowledge, understanding and forms of thought with curriculum content (Nutbrown, 1994, pp. 61–113). If we recognise the importance of knowing about children in order to help them with their learning, it is worth thinking about how we come to know them. We can use two approaches simultaneously: learning what we can about child development and children's learning generally, and learning what we can about each individual child (Bartholomew and Bruce, 1993).

Partnership between parents and staff

When it comes to getting to know individual children, their most important people – usually their parents – are the experts. The adults who live with and care for a child day after day, night after night, will have an accumulation of knowledge and understanding about that child which teachers can never hope to match (Whalley, 1994, pp. 61–2).

Staff in early childhood education settings and in primary schools may have learned a good deal about child development in their training and will have a body of experience to support their theoretical knowledge (Lally, 1991, pp. 94–6). Child development is about all aspects of a child's development: emotional, social and cognitive, as well as physical. It is only after a certain amount of training and experience that it becomes possible to differentiate between the 'normal' and the 'special' in children's behaviour and development. Staff with a wide range of experience, together with theoretical knowledge of 'normality', are able to recognise reliably what is 'normal' and what is 'special'.

Parents know best what is normal behaviour for their own children and what signals illness or upset. They can gain a great deal from books, papers and articles, too, but such reading usually applies to a *range* of real-life children, and what is 'normal' for one child may not be for another. Staff are therefore able to help parents check their perceptions of their children in the wider context. Another strategy that parents can, and often do, use is to watch other people's children and to make comparisons. This can be very useful as a means of identifying interests and patterns of learning; it works well when used as a way of focusing on what children *can* do. Much less useful is when comparisons are made unfavourably with other children, without taking developmental factors into account. Often this results in too high expectations, which most children find overwhelming.

We can make our knowledge and understanding work for children by developing alliances between parents and staff. These alliances are based on combining parents' knowledge of the child as an individual and staff knowledge of child development and children's learning in general. This is best done right from the beginning, from the first time a child enters a new learning environment away from the home. With an expectation of partnership on both sides, and with an attitude of give-and-take, parents and staff can use each other's knowledge and understanding to support the child's learning (Whalley, 1994, pp. 13–18). This is the bedrock of real home–school partnership.

Observing children

How do we get to know children? Using our eyes and ears seems an obvious and simple answer. But watching and listening to children is indeed of the utmost importance (Hurst, in Moyles, 1994, pp. 173–88). Often, however, we are under such pressure to get things done that stopping to watch and listen is much harder than it sounds. Parents of older children usually wish they had spent more time watching and listening to their young children, and members of staff frequently wish they had more time for observation of individual children.

Grandparents who are fortunate enough to have close contact with their grandchildren without the burden of round-the-clock care say that among the greatest pleasures are the opportunities to watch and listen. The fact that they are able to do that may account for the very special, close relationships that often develop between children and their grandparents.

The problem is not only one of time. So many of us, wholly understandably, do not fully realise the value and the need for watching and listening to children with detailed care and attention. The trouble is that we are often unaware of the gaps in our knowledge, and our understanding will always be partial. But nevertheless five or ten minutes of an adult's absolutely undivided attention on one child can be amazingly clarifying. There are also numerous occasions during the day at home and at school when the actions, feelings and talk of children may be seen or heard with attention, and accepted, by adults; or alternatively may pass unnoticed.

Careful watching involves an eye for detail and the exercise of curiosity. A great deal can be learned, particularly about feelings and attitudes, simply from watching children's body language when they are with each other or with other adults. Watching carefully over a period of time enables an adult to gain insights into *why* children behave as they do and what particular events cause certain reactions.

How useful to discover that Lily concentrates particularly well at nursery on days when she has been able to say goodbye to Mum in a thorough and unhurried way, and to notice that Joe only does that sudden loud screaming that they couldn't understand when Mum *sits down* to talk to someone else. How reassuring and comforting for Lily when her 'important people' realise that saying goodbye properly really matters to her and do so accordingly; and how soothing for Joe to find that when Mum sits down to talk to people, she scoops him onto her lap so that he feels part of the conversation and can get down and go off to play when he wants to.

In particular, listening carefully to what children say and talking with them 'conversationally' rather than 'instructionally' is a revealing and rewarding process. Also – although it may sound like eavesdropping – the conversations that children have with each other or with another adult can be just as instructive as the conversations we have with them ourselves. Whether or not this is an invasion of their privacy may depend on *why* we watch and listen; occasionally to do so genuinely in order to understand children better, and thereby to support and care for them more appropriately, seems entirely valid.

The quality and usefulness of observations in early childhood education settings can depend on the ways in which they are recorded and used. A variety of possibilities can be considered (Bartholomew and Bruce, 1993, pp. 25–68). Watching and listening to children really carefully means that new experiences can be planned to connect with their existing knowledge and understanding. We know that this way of supporting and extending children's learning matches the learning process. It ensures that we do not waste precious time providing experiences at an inappropriate level. In addition, children's 'important people' are more likely to have *realistically* high expectations of them. This means that children are more liable to find themselves in situations which are just right for optimal learning: neither overwhelming nor lacking in challenge.

Behind the stereotypes

Some children who find life overwhelming are thought to be shy, anxious or even lazy. These children cannot seem to get on with things in the way that other children do. They watch a lot, hovering on the edge of other children's activities, either avoiding contact with adults or heavily dependent on them. Sometimes they seem to be oblivious to things around them and sometimes they will only play with a very few familiar things, unwilling to risk anything new.

Something is holding these children back from living their lives to the full. Often that something is an overload in their lives, of things that they cannot make sense of, or even begin to understand. They are incapacitated by too much struggling with the incomprehensible; nor do they have sufficient relevant and assimilated experiences to combine with new knowledge and understanding.

The trouble with verdicts like 'shy', 'anxious' and 'lazy' is that they describe a child's state without necessarily looking for causes. However, a 'shy' child may be affected by the sheer number of unknown people in his or her environment. An 'anxious' child may be struggling with an excessive amount of uncertainty. A 'lazy' child may be unable to respond to the level of expectation that he or she perceives is being demanded. Children who appear to fit these descriptions may, in fact, feel overwhelmed; asking ourselves the questions 'Overwhelmed by what?' and 'How can the pressure be eased?' may be more helpful than our usual responses to these characteristics.

– JOE AT NURSERY –

❝ Mum had a work problem this week and couldn't be with Joe in the mornings.

Usually on Lily's nursery day, I take Lily and Mum stays at home with Joe. Mum said did I think I could manage to look after Joe for her by taking him to nursery? Or would it be better if I stayed at home just this week? In the end, we decided that he'd probably like it at nursery and that, now Lily's really settled down, I could keep an eye on him as well as being a bit of a help to the other children sometimes.

Well, it was the hardest morning ever! Once or twice I thought we were going to have to give up and go home. Joe absolutely loved it, but he couldn't wait to find out about everything, so as soon as he'd started doing something, he was off to the next thing. The teacher was really understanding; as soon as she saw Joe, she said she was really glad he'd come, but that I'd better spend the morning keeping an eye on him and not try to do anything else. She looked pleased when I said he didn't put things in his mouth all the time any more.

Once, I stopped for a minute to help Michael do up his shoes. I thought Joe was happy standing on a box pouring water into a giant bottle in the water tray, but when I'd done the shoe, Joe had vanished. In the end, I found him on the other side of the garden at the top of the scramble net. He was really pleased to be at the top, but he couldn't get down because his shoe was caught in the rope. As soon as I'd lifted him down, he wanted to climb up again, but that time he didn't get stuck.

It was very muddy in the garden from all the rain, and there was a huge puddle that the children were riding the bikes through, lifting up their feet so they didn't get wet. Of course, Joe didn't know how to lift his feet up, so we had to go and find a dry pair of trousers in the cupboard. Then he wanted to do the fingerpainting in the workshop. I don't know how he managed to get the paint up past his elbows and into his hair. The teacher laughed and said he'd done a really thorough job. She said she liked seeing children having a go at things.

Joe didn't learn from the puddle mistake, though, although he did learn that it was fun to go whizzing through puddles. He loved it so much that he had another go when I thought he was playing in the sandpit, and got wet all over again! In the end, I decided that it wouldn't hurt him to be a bit wet as it wasn't cold, so I left him. It was just as well I hadn't changed him again – next he found the little blue paddling pool full of earth and water; and had a wonderful time making mud pies. When it was time to go home he looked like a mud pie himself, and I spent all afternoon washing muddy clothes while he had his sleep. As soon as he woke up, he wanted to go again! ❞

Some learning skills come naturally; these include exploring, questioning, experimenting and learning from mistakes

Encouraging exploratory learning

The essentially exploring nature of young children is recognised as being crucial to their learning (Isaacs, 1954, pp. 20–1). However, living with exploring children of this age is a major challenge. There is a constant need to strike the right balance between challenge and safety. Children need to be encouraged to explore, discover and learn from their mistakes. They need to find out about their world and about the consequences of their actions in it. But, at the same time, they must be protected from physical danger and from extreme distress.

It is not easy to get this balance right. Adequate safety is easy to remember, with the threat of dangerous consequences; children are more secure when clear boundaries have been defined about when, where and how they can explore, question and try things out. Allowing young children enough exploration may be harder, especially as it can sometimes result in a certain amount of inconvenience. It can be helpful to remember that questioning and exploring are *natural* activities for young children.

There are three important things that we can do to meet children's needs for exploratory activity: ensure they have enough *time* to explore, enough *space* and enough *attention* (Singer and Singer, 1990, pp. 153–75). Children's lives all too often tend to reflect the pace of their parents', and for some, this means a busy life. Exploring is not just about rushing around doing things; it is also about watching, listening and reflecting. Sometimes, when children appear to be doing nothing, they are actually working very hard at the process of exploration.

As well as time, children need enough space: to move around, to make choices, to allow a measure of independence from the nearest adult. This can be difficult to achieve in crowded families and small play areas and classrooms. Where 'playing out' is no longer safe, the provision of play areas that *are* safe for children should be high on the agenda of new building developments and of communities able to improve their facilities.

The third dimension that we can give children is our attention – to deal with questions honestly, to make time to find out about their interests and intentions, and to help them think confidently about their successes and mistakes. They need our attention in listening, valuing, questioning and encouraging; and they need our commitment to provide a variety of interesting, relevant experiences in which they can be actively involved.

Setting examples for children

A question which crops up time and again is: what sort of role models are we for children? Do *we* explore, experiment and learn from mistakes? It is hard to overestimate the influence we have in this respect. Children need our acceptance and approval, and they try to be like their 'important adults'. If we always have the right answer, children get the idea that it is never all right not to know. If we never try something out unless we know that it will work, our implicit message to them is, 'Don't risk it'. If our attitude to failure is to hide and deny it, how will they learn to accept and think about their mistakes in order to do things better next time?

We all know children and adults – maybe sometimes ourselves among them – who rarely go looking for something new, who always have an answer, who never risk making a mistake. How did we get like that? What altered our naturally exploring, experimenting early childhood characters? Pressure to 'get things right' is increasing. Both in homes and outside, there is more awareness of the very real dangers and consequences of doing things wrong; and in schools, there is greater pressure for assessment of skills, knowledge and understanding, rather than of effort and progress.

Accurate assessment is, of course, crucial for high quality teaching; good teachers have always been aware of this and welcome opportunities to sharpen their focus. But we need to be very vigilant about the messages we give to children about 'right' and 'wrong' answers if we are to continue to nurture their natural learning skills (Drummond, 1993, p. 95). The pressures to 'get it right' are the very pressures that threaten to impair children's ability to think creatively and learn effectively. In all areas of their lives, the ability to remember facts will indeed be useful; but the habit of trying out solutions, the knowledge that mistakes are a normal part of learning, and the attitude that accepts and uses them positively, will be crucial.

Of course, there are occasions when we need to get things as 'right' as possible: for instance, in examinations, important public events, celebrations for other people. But these are 'one-offs'. Day by day, together with consistent effort, what counts in successful learning are habits of reasonably safe exploration, experimentation and reflection. Accepting and using both success *and* failure is what serves learning best.

– PRETEND PAINTING –

❝ There's a big change in Aisha at the nursery these days. When she first came, she didn't do anything much, especially not on her own or with the other children. She always had to be with the teacher and she only liked making things to take home. She didn't play with anything else much or do any exploring. She was kind of opposite to how Joe was that day he came to nursery.

I think the teacher decided it was time to persuade Aisha that it was OK to go and try things out and make a few mistakes, and even make a bit of a mess sometimes – so long as she helps to clear it up. Maybe she needed to persuade Aisha's mum, too. One day the teacher asked Aisha's mum if she could drop in for a cup of tea on the way home, and her mum was really pleased. She said Aisha could show her her favourite toys, and that she would buy a special cake, but the teacher said she was on a diet!

Anyway, ever since then Aisha has been different. Yesterday was really good. Omar and Lily had made a camp by hanging an old sheet over two tables so they could get underneath; but they wanted one side of the sheet to lift up higher so their camp could have a sort of outside bit. Once before the teacher had made a camp like that by tying bits of string to two corners of the sheet and fixing the string to hooks on the wall. Aisha must have seen her because she went off and asked for string, and she got the scissors and she did just the same thing. The others thought it was really clever of her and I did too; I had to help her with the tying, but I'd forgotten about doing that until she remembered.

Then I was even more surprised, because soon after that, she went and did pretend painting with Lily and Omar and another boy called Saleem. Mum told me that Saleem's dad comes from Pakistan, and that at home they speak Punjabi as well as English, so Saleem can talk in both languages. He must be so pleased he can do that. Anyway, they do pretend painting sometimes when it's hot. They had the great big paint brushes and buckets of water and they were pretending to be decorators coming to paint the play house in the den. I think Omar must have seen a real painter at home or somewhere, because he kept stirring up the water and sloshing it on with the real up-and-down strokes. It all got a bit wild, and they were giggling and getting wet, and in a minute I thought they'd be painting each other so I said, 'Isn't it time for your tea break?' And Aisha said to Omar, 'Do you take sugar?' Then she pretended it was her house and went inside to make the tea; and Lily pretended to be the boss and told Omar his painting wasn't very good and he'd have to do it again.

Aisha came back with pretend tea on a tray from the home corner and they decided to have it in the camp – and all that time Aisha didn't seem to worry about making a mess or fetching things they needed. Perhaps she's changed her mind about what nursery's for – I think it must have helped that her teacher came to her house for tea. **'**

In order to be 'socially acceptable', children often learn to behave in ways that inhibit learning

Factors inhibiting learning

Our dilemma is that we all want our children to be successful learners; but we also want to help them to fit into families and society, which seems to mean less exploring and more restraint about their feelings. We may feel, particularly outside the home, that the two traits of exploring and of expressing negative feelings as well as positive ones are indeed unacceptable. If so, must we then 'give up' on those two crucial aspects of children's learning?

It can be argued that children are liable to be cognitively disabled without the development of exploratory learning skills. It can also be argued that giving up on children's ability to acknowledge and express – and thereby begin to resolve – feelings of pain, fear and anger also carries major penalties. If we fail to acknowledge a child's need to resolve these feelings, then the child may consequently lack determination, clarity and confidence; and these characteristics – so vital in many aspects of living – are also needed in order to develop as an exploratory learner.

Studies which focus on this dilemma are reported by Sylva (in Ball, 1994, pp. 91–4). Children are categorised as 'mastery' children and 'helpless' children. Here is her summary of the results:

- *Helpless children avoid challenge and give up easily, whereas mastery-oriented children persist in the face of obstacles and seek new, challenging experiences.*
- *Helpless children report negative feelings and views of themselves when they meet obstacles, while 'mastery' children have positive views of their competence and enjoy challenges.*
- *The style of 'helpless'- or 'mastery'-oriented behaviour is not related to intelligence; rather, it is a personality characteristic, a way of viewing oneself and one's capacity to be effective with things and people.*

This issue about 'mastery' and 'helplessness' is an important factor. We know that children are naturally active, learning best by exploring, questioning and experimenting. We also know that the most sociable and successful children are those who manage to *combine* their exploratory learning with an awareness of others. However, in the previously mentioned study about the development of children's self-perception (Roberts, 1993, p. 64), it emerged that a majority of the children in the study did not see themselves as exploratory, but preferred to think of themselves as receptive.

Two groups were particularly significant, where the children were almost unanimous in seeing themselves as receptive. One was a group from a particularly disadvantaged housing estate; the other was a group whose parents had very high expectations of their children. It appeared that, at four years old, both these groups of children had already learned – for very different reasons – that to risk getting things wrong was too dangerous. They could no longer imagine themselves behaving in a 'normal' exploratory way. Here again, we are seeing what happens when children feel overwhelmed. There may not be a great deal we can do about the causes, but what we can do is recognise children's feelings and responses, and make sure that they do have the opportunities for safe exploration that they need.

Staff and parents need to work together to clarify for children the expectations of adults in those special places where children go to learn. Children need to know that schools are unique places, different from home, but also different from being 'out' in the general sense. They need to know that in schools they are expected to take a measure of ownership and a measure of responsibility; that exploring and expressing feelings is both necessary and desirable; that it is safe to be themselves as deeply and widely as they can; and that they will learn about their place as an individual within a group.

Obviously it is important that children do learn to behave in ways that are socially acceptable – but there is more to be done. Schools should be places where it is safe to explore and experiment, where making mistakes is seen as normal and useful, and where questions and discussions are encouraged. Many would argue that this happens already; particularly when it is their *intention* that children should feel this way about school. However, we do need to question children's actual perceptions about appropriate learning behaviour at school (Pascal, 1990, p. 32).

For most children, the places where they go to learn will never feel as safe as home. But we must make sure that children know that schools are *relatively* safe places in which to explore and make mistakes, and that the children themselves know this. An effective way to work on this re-definition of schools is by setting our own examples. If we, as staff and parents, are willing to value ourselves and each other, to try things out when we are uncertain of the result, to celebrate successes and mistakes and be honest about our feelings, children are likely to follow our lead. Changing the habits of a lifetime may be hard, but the results for children would be worth the struggle.

POSTSCRIPT TO PART 4: LINKING WITH LEARNING

Living or working with young children?
Questions to think about . . .

> Learning involves struggle and adjustment. Too much struggle is overwhelming. Too little struggle means no adjustment

1. How do we form our expectations of children? What can we do to try and make sure they are appropriate?

> Some learning skills come naturally; these include exploring, questioning, experimenting and learning from mistakes

2. How good are we at modeling learning skills for children? Do they see us exploring, questioning, experimenting and learning from mistakes?

> In order to be 'socially acceptable', children often learn to behave in ways that inhibit learning

3. What social behaviours do we expect of children? And what learning behaviours? Are these expectations compatible, or do children sometimes receive mixed messages from their 'important adults' about what is expected of them?

RECOMMENDED FURTHER READING

For sharing with children . . .

Waddell, M. and Firth, B. (1999), *Well Done, Little Bear,* **London, Walker Books**
Another lovely book from Martin Waddell, this one is about a young learner, Little Bear, exploring and learning from mistakes. The loving adult, Big Bear, encourages, supports, rescues, comforts, allows herself (or himself, it could very satisfactorily be either) to be led, and finally talks with Little Bear about the adventure. This is a satisfying picture of the parent–child relationship, offering a security that comforts adult and child alike.

Ahlberg, J. and A. (1978), *Each Peach Pear Plum,* **London, Puffin Books**
All the Ahlberg books are brilliant, and this one is no exception. It is an exquisite 'I Spy' game, with a cast of childhood favourites – Tom Thumb, Mother Hubbard, Cinderella, the Three Bears, Baby Bunting, Jack and Jill, the Wicked Witch and Robin Hood – and swinging rhyme and rhythm. And best of all, it ends with a wonderful picnic feast!

. . . and for a good read

Siraj-Blatchford, I. and Clarke, P. (2000), *Supporting Identity, Diversity and Language in the Early Years,* **Buckingham, Open University Press**
Here is a wonderful book about working with young children in a diverse society. It links with sections in this book on identity, self-concept and self-esteem, exploring these concepts from a multi-cultural perspective which is enormously helpful and effective. There are important chapters about language acquisition, and a very helpful chapter on parents as partners. The book is an excellent combination of theory and practice, both well informed and extremely helpful on a practical level.

PART 5

REAL SELF-ESTEEM

9

Children's successful learning

– LILY AND JOE'S PICNIC –

❛ Lily's just got a new buggy for her two dolls, and there's a place underneath where she can put things like pretend picnics for them. She used to play picnics with the little old truck that was for the wooden bricks, but now she's given that to Joe. He's really pleased – he puts things in it and wheels it about; but he's having to learn how to steer it. It's easier for him to pull it than push it, but he doesn't like doing that because then he isn't doing it like Lily.

Lily and Joe had a great game outside today. Lily decided to take her dolls for a walk, and Joe trailed along after. He made a fuss at first, because there wasn't anything in his truck, but Lily dropped in some old bits of Duplo that were on the floor, and then he was quite happy. I don't think he realised that the game was about dolls; he just wanted to wheel his truck with something in it.

When they came to the big tree, Lily propped up the dolls on the grass by the trunk and emptied out all the bits and pieces from underneath the buggy. Joe just watched. Lily looked at the dolls thoughtfully. Then she said they were hungry and she'd have to go to the shop because there wasn't enough to eat. 'They'd better have a sleep,' she said, busily laying them down and tucking the little blanket over them. 'Stay there, children – I won't be long!' she said in her grown-up voice. Then she grabbed the handle of the buggy and went off back towards the house. 'I have to make a shopping list,' she muttered to herself as she passed me.

Joe tried to get the truck to go forwards like Lily did with the buggy, but the wheels wouldn't work because they were covered in mud. I showed him how to scrape the mud off one wheel with a stick; and then I said he could do the rest. He wanted me to do it for him, but I said I'd watch, and if he really couldn't do it, I'd help him. So he had a go at the others; and he did it quite well, so after that the truck worked. He was really pleased with himself.

Lily had found an old list of Mum's and added some writing of her own. 'This says "special cheese and Dinocrackers and apples",' she told me and Joe. Dinocrackers are her favourites. I asked her where the shop was. 'There,' she said, pointing to the store-cupboard that Mum was clearing out.

'I hope you've got some money, then!' Mum said. She was just coming out with a load of old boxes and packets.

'We need a picnic,' said Lily firmly, holding out the list. Joe edged up a bit nearer. Mum said they could have some of the boxes she was throwing away, for pretending, and they'd need something to put them in. She said Lily would have to make sure that Joe didn't eat anything because it was all a bit old and he might get a tummy-ache.

They spent ages going backwards and forwards between the store-cupboard and the kitchen with empty and half-full boxes, bags, trays and baskets. After a bit, Joe got fed up with trailing backwards and forwards carrying things; he had a great time instead standing on the big tree root throwing all the empty boxes down into his truck. Then he found a cereal packet with some old cereal left in the bottom; and he was just putting a handful in his mouth when Lily spotted him. She hadn't forgotten what Mum had said, so with one hand she grabbed the box and with the other Joe's hand with the old cereal in it. Of course, there was a struggle, and Joe screamed and Lily shouted and Joe pulled her hair, all in half a minute.

When I'd dragged them apart, I said to Lily that she'd have to think of a clever way to stop Joe eating the old cereal, not just grab it off him. Joe looked as if he was going to start screaming again, so I sat him on my knee and told him Lily had something very special to tell him – and then we looked at Lily to see what she would say. Lily looked at Joe, and then she looked at the old box, and then she said, 'You can have some new cereal in a bowl if you like.' Then she pointed towards the house, and Joe got off my lap, and they went off to find it.

Lily got her dolls all sorted out in the end. She made them sit up and eat their picnic, and then she told them a long story about a magic rabbit that lived underneath the tree. I think it was the one that her dad told her last week; Joe thought it was really good at first, but after a bit he pushed off with his truck. When Mum saw the mess under the tree, she said she had sorted out all the boxes and things once and she wasn't going to do it all over again. She gave us a rubbish bag and said if I held it open, Lily could put all the boxes in, now the dolls had had their picnic. Lily really liked putting everything in the bag – she was so keen, I thought she might put the dolls in too, but then she said it was time they had a rest in their cots. She walked off towards the house dragging the rubbish bag behind her, with a couple of little blankets in the other hand, and the two dolls tucked carefully one under each arm. **9**

Children are encouraged to learn when someone knows what they especially want to do and can nearly manage, and helps them to manage it successfully

Learning and play

Encouraging and helping young children to learn must be one of the most fundamental of our tasks as 'important adults'. Three factors can be helpful here. First, we need to think about how young children go about learning; second, we need to identify the most effective things we can do to help them; and third, we need to understand ways in which realistic, high self-esteem can be achieved.

These are the main issues in these two chapters, and although the sections deal with various separate aspects for the sake of clarity, the issues are, in reality, all interwoven and interdependent. The whole picture is viewed through the perspective of the child's self-esteem, which is seen as the key to balanced development and learning.

Young children learn effectively in a number of ways. These include exploring, observing and listening, representing first-hand experiences in a variety of ways, and play involving a combination of ideas, feelings and relationships with the application of skills and competence. Playing and talking are, for young children, two principal means of bringing together a range of these activities.

It is often said that children learn through play; there is, however, less agreement about exactly what is meant by play. Bruce (1991, p. 3) illuminates the debate about play by describing the two main categories of play theory as 'play versus work' theories and 'play as education' theories. 'Play versus work' theories define play negatively in terms of what it is not (e.g. not work). The 'play as education' strand, dealing with play as preparation for life, tends to see it as preconceived and dominated by adults, who, of course, know what life holds in store. There may, however, be particular concern about preparing for the future at the expense of meeting children's current needs.

It is the 'play as an integrating mechanism' model – referred to by Bruce as 'free-flow play' – that best enables the creative end result of previous struggle and practice. The characteristics of free-flow play as described by Bruce allow for the combination of ideas, feelings and relationships (intention) with the application of competence and technical prowess (knowledge and skill). When children (or adults) are using this combination of intention and knowledge and skill, they are playing – or working – creatively. It would be helpful if the word 'play' were only used to refer to this essentially creative process. At every level, from sensory-motor babyhood to the most abstract adult thought, it is new *combinations* of understanding from which new hypotheses are formed and new discoveries are made. This is when 'the penny drops', when the wonderful 'eureka' moments occur. Indeed, it could be said that children learn – by watching, listening, exploring and representing their experiences, gaining knowledge and understanding and developing skills – primarily in order to play. All these aspects of learning culminate in play.

It follows, therefore, that providing children with opportunities to play (creatively to use their own intentions, understanding, knowledge and competence) is ensuring learning at the point where it becomes fun. Children who can play at home and who have had the benefit of quality early childhood education settings are generally eager to learn, cheerfully responsive and full of curiosity. They thrive on a balance of exploration, developing knowledge and skills, together with any opportunities to experience the fundamental satisfaction of playing creatively.

For many children, however, such settings are not available. Donaldson (1978, p. 14) suggested that large numbers of children:

> . . . leave school with the bitter taste of defeat in them, not having mastered even moderately well those basic skills which society demands, much less having become people who rejoice in the exercise of creative intelligence.

It must be acknowledged that this is still liable to be true in the twenty-first century; and although the reasons are becoming ever more complex and interrelated, it can be strongly argued that one reason for this is a lack of recognition of the value of free-flow play, in and beyond the Foundation Stage. As children grow older, time for play (in the creative sense), both in the classroom and at home, is usually curtailed. Many children who continue to learn do so for extrinsic reasons, such as reward systems, testing or the need for adult approval. Unfortunately, however, these reasons for learning seldom stand the test of time. Research into the benefits of early childhood education (Sylva, in Ball, 1994, pp. 84–94) has shown that the effects of well-assimilated skills, knowledge and understanding stay with children and positively affect their lives. Well-assimilated learning can be used in creative combinations bringing pleasure and the intrinsic motivation to learn more.

Supporting children's efforts

A crucially important idea in relation to encouraging and supporting children's learning is about identifying and focusing on what children can *nearly* do. This area of children's development is seen as distinct from the area of development on which we usually focus: what children can do on their own without help. In planning for children's learning, it has been our practice to measure children's knowledge, understanding and competence in order to determine at what level we may best help them. In the past, it has been generally assumed that anything a child needed help with did not count for assessment; in fact, to include in an assessment of a child's learning something that he or she needed help with felt like cheating. Currently we have begun to see the implications of the proposition (Vygotsky, 1978, p. 86) that, in planning to support children's learning, we should focus primarily on those things that children can *nearly* do on their own, rather than using as our starting-points the things they can already do without help.

Clearly this proposition makes sense. Knowing the actual levels of development and achievement that children have reached is certainly important. But all children are not going to learn exactly the same things and in a standard order. Knowledge about what children have already learned tells us nothing at all about what children are *currently* engaged in learning. We will surely help children to learn more effectively by focusing on what they want and are trying to do and what they can begin to manage with a bit of help and encouragement from someone who is at least a few steps ahead.

In relation to finding out more about a child's ability, Vygotsky suggests that it is the rate at which a child can cover the ground between the level of doing something now with help and the level of doing it independently which tells us most about the child's current potential. The area between those two levels is the cutting edge of each child's learning – Vygotsky's name for it is 'the zone of proximal development'. How long will it take Joe to learn to find a stick and scrape the mud off the wheels of his truck without anyone suggesting it or helping him? Will Lily be able to use what she learned about managing Joe to handle a similar situation on her own tomorrow? or next week? or next year? The answers to these questions would tell us more about Joe and Lily's future ability to learn than would a couple of statements such as, 'Joe can scrape mud off wheels' or 'Lily can manage Joe'.

Helping children to help themselves

If we want to be really effective in helping children in their learning, we need to be thinking, day by day, about what it is that they are *trying* to do; and about what it is they *could* do, with a little help from us. This process of supporting children in their learning until they can manage on their own is sometimes referred to as 'scaffolding' learning (Bruner and Haste, 1987, pp. 21–2). Scaffolding, in the learning context, implies the use of talking and listening by an adult or more able child, in order to support the learners' efforts. So when Joe needed to make the truck work, he was supported by encouragement and offers of help if he needed it; and when Lily needed to sort out Joe, she was supported by the expectation that she would think of something appropriate and effective – which she did. The help that Lily received from Mum that morning made it easier for Lily to do things that she either wanted or needed to do: Mum supplied Lily with boxes for her game at the very point at which she needed them, and Mum suggested a way of clearing up that would appeal to Lily.

The idea of 'scaffolding' is akin to the ideas of 'holding' and 'containment' which were considered earlier in this book. Some of those practical suggestions, for instance about acceptance and role modelling, apply here too. Thinking back to our own learning experiences (such as, for instance, our early days of living and working with children), how important was it to us to receive support? What was the most helpful kind of support we received from others with more experience, as we found our feet? Were we conscious of progressing from needing support to managing on our own? The answers to these questions may provide some insight into the implications of Vygotsky's ideas about ways to support children's learning.

– MOVING HOUSE –

❛ *I saw Lily's new friend at nursery today. She's called Henna, and Lily has been talking about her all week. When we got to nursery, Henna hadn't arrived yet, and the teacher asked Lily if she'd like to help get the things out of the shed in the garden; but Lily shook her head and waited by the door till Henna came.*

I was really surprised when I saw Henna. I thought she was going to be sparkly and full of beans, the way Lily talked about her. But she was little and quiet. She smiled a huge smile when she saw Lily waiting for her, but she didn't say anything. She and her mum had come with Nerinda and Imran and their mums, and they were all busy talking together, so Lily and Henna went off into the playroom, to the home corner.

I had to go and help with the children in the paddling pool in the garden, so I didn't see them for a while. When I went back to the home corner to look for them, they'd gone – and so had nearly all the things in the home corner! It turned out that they were playing 'moving house' and they'd made another house just outside by the woodwork bench. There's a big table there, and the teacher had given them a blanket to put over it, and they'd made the new house inside.

It was quite crowded in there, but really neat. They had the little cooker, the cupboard, and all the cutlery and the pretend food. They had a blanket for a bed as well, and it was folded over so you could get inside. They even had the telephone! One of the mums told me that Lily had done most of the fetching and carrying, and Henna was the one who sorted things out. When the teacher said it was nearly time to clear up, I thought Lily would make an awful fuss, but she didn't; Henna was really organised, and they went backwards and forwards quite happily until it was all done.

When I told Lily's dad about it in the evening, he laughed and said Lily sounded like his mate who does a delivery job, and perhaps Lily will end up driving lorries too! And Mum said she'd rather Lily was more like Henna, then she'd be better at putting her toys back in the cupboard and shutting the door, instead of leaving them all over the house. ❜

Recognising and supporting the development of children's patterns of learning, or schemas, leads to high self-esteem

Children's patterns of learning (schemas)

Kant first wrote about the idea of schemas 250 years ago, calling it schematism (Walsh, in Wolff, 1968, pp. 71–87). Much later, Piaget (1953) illustrated schemas from the earliest co-ordinations right through to the symbolic co-ordinating of symbolic functioning. Comprehensive and clarifying work on schemas is to be found in Athey's book (1990), which describes the Froebel project study. Bruce (1991) and Nutbrown (1994) have written about schemas, showing how an awareness of them can be used to support and extend children's learning. Much work about schemas has been done by parents and staff together, particularly at Redford House Nursery at Roehampton University in London (Bartholomew and Bruce, 1993) and at the Pen Green Centre for Families and Children Under Five in Corby, Northamptonshire (Whalley, 1994). The PEEP project makes these ideas accessible to parents and carers in the PEEP 'Learning Together' series (Roberts, (ed.) 2000a), especially in the Summer section of 'Learning Together with Threes'.

The recognition and development of children's schemas – or patterns of learning – can be a key to effective ways of helping children to learn, and to raise their self-esteem. Schemas are, simply, patterns of repeatable behaviour in children. We have seen, for instance, a strong pattern in Lily's play in relation to moving things from one place to another. Lily's strong schema at the moment is about 'transporting'. Lily's friend Henna has a different pattern: her play shows that she loves covering things up and putting things into other things. Her schemas are enveloping and containing.

These patterns are likely to run through everything that Lily and Henna do at the moment. For instance, Lily loves being asked to serve out at tea-time, which involves transferring food from dish to plate; and she often takes her mattress off her bed and re-makes it on the other side of the room or even out on the landing. She loves board games like Lotto and Snakes and Ladders that involve moving counters horizontally and vertically, and her favourite treat is a journey of any sort.

Henna's play reflects different patterns. Her best toy as a toddler was a posting box, and her favourite game was when her mum put a cot sheet right over the top of her cot, and she had a cosy den inside. Henna spends long periods at the water tray filling up jugs and bottles, and when she gets a new toy, she's more likely to play with the box it came in than with the toy itself.

Lily's friend Dan is a 'trajectory' child. He loves running, jumping, throwing and kicking – in fact, anything involving lines and movement. Later on, unless his schemas change dramatically, he might well be especially interested in guns, bows and arrows and rockets; he loves the garden games at nursery, like 'hit the bottle', the punch bag, skittles, and the goal posts.

The construction sets, the train track, and gluing are favourite activities for Michael and Jessica. These two love joining things together, so they have a passion for string and Sellotape, laying wooden bricks end to end in a long line, and hanging up washing with clothes pegs. The schema these share is connection.

Amy is especially interested in circle games, roundabouts and things with wheels; she loves watching the clothes going round in the washing machine, and one week she was fascinated by the concrete mixer outside the nursery. Her schema is rotation.

Although children often show particular schemas in their play, not all children appear especially schematic. Some show one schema particularly strongly, and others show several at once. Sometimes one schema that has been particularly strong will seem to fade, possibly to be replaced by another.

Sometimes the results of young children's play seem particularly messy or destructive. Glue gets in the wrong place, contents of drawers and cupboards are transferred to other places, things are thrown, furniture is jumped on – or off! Some schemas, such as 'transporting' and 'trajectory' play, are often inconvenient, both at home and at school. An insight into the schematic compulsions at the heart of this sort of play can help us to provide for children's needs in a more manageable way. Doing this avoids much frustration for adults and gives considerable satisfaction to children. For instance, the provision of an old shopping basket and some empty boxes and tins will go a long way to prevent the apparently random redistribution of other, more precious, objects; and there is a wide range of alternatives, from instruction in the making of paper aeroplanes to the provision of an old mattress specially for bouncing, which will meet the needs of the 'trajectory' child, whose interests include throwing and jumping.

One of the most valuable aspects of providing for schematic activity is that, in doing so, we are recognising and valuing children's fundamental interests and needs. This is a powerful way of genuinely raising children's self-esteem. Instead of the likelihood of disapproval for playing in ways that seem normal and natural to them, we can make provision for children to play in the ways that they need to, safely and acceptably. In this way, we are letting children know that we accept how they are and what they want to do. In the warmth of approval, positive self-concept thrives.

– BUILDING A DEN –

❝ *Last week there was a special day at the nursery when everyone went to help. It was a good thing that it was on my Saturday off, so I didn't miss it. They called it 'Gardening and Mending Day', and it was so that lots of things got mended and sorted out.*

They'd started to plan it the week before, so I knew a bit about it already. First, they made a list of all the jobs that needed doing and the problems that needed sorting out. I don't remember all of them, but it was things like mending the fence where the hole is and putting the wheels back on the cart. As well as mending things, they wanted to make some new things for the children in the garden, like a pulley in the tree, for hauling things up and down, and a washing line for hanging up dolls' clothes when the children have washed them. Another thing they wanted was a special place where the children could make dens and tents out of old sheets and bits of string, but without starting right from the beginning every time; so it needed some hooks in the right places and somewhere to store the string and sheets and things.

The list of things was on the notice board, so you could sign up for what you wanted to do. I really liked the sound of the place for dens, and I knew Lily would love it, too, so that's what I signed up for. They said that children could help too if they liked; or they could play so long as they kept out of the way.

It was a lovely day, which was lucky because we had a picnic, and there wouldn't have been room for everyone inside if it had rained. Mum said it would be best if Joe stayed at home with her; she thought it would be easier for everyone, and she said she didn't want him getting covered in the red paint they were going to paint the home corner with! On the way, Lily wanted to know what we were going to do, and I told her about sorting out how to make a den. I was right, she wanted to know all about how we could make it stay up. I said I didn't know, and that we'd have to think about that when we were doing it.

When we got there, it was really busy. Lily's friend Dan was there; his mum and dad were mending the trucks, and so was Imran's dad. The teacher gave me the things to make the den with and showed me where she wanted it. I told Lily I thought it would be great if she could help me, and the teacher said Lily was just the person to sort it out, so off we went. Dan and Imran came too; Dan said they could play in the den when we'd made it, and Lily said he'd have to help make it then.

The place was under the tree that the children climb in, near the swing. The teacher said we could use the little wooden climbing frame, if we wanted. She'd given us hooks, nappy pins, three old sheets, a ball of string and some clothes pegs. She also said that she thought there were a couple of tent poles in the shed, and they might be useful.

It was really good that the children helped, because they knew what they wanted; if it had been only me, I wouldn't have done it the same at all. First of all, we sat on the grass and talked about dens and what you want them for. Dan said they were for hiding, so they had to have a roof and be dark, and Lily said they had to have two doors, one for going in and one for getting out. Imran said they were for eating things in, and Lily said, 'And for milk'. Then Imran said baddies aren't allowed, and the others agreed. I asked who was a baddie, and they looked at each other a bit ashamed and didn't say anything. I know the teacher doesn't like them talking about baddies; once I heard her saying they use it as a way of keeping some children out of their games, and that's unkind to those children.

We talked about how big to make it and how to hold it up. They thought using the climbing frame would be best, but when we got it out, we found it wouldn't go under the lowest branch of the tree, so that was no good. Then they said we could hold it up with string, and so we tied one end to the branch – but there was nothing to hold up the other end. Lily thought we could just put it over another branch, but then she said the den wouldn't be big enough for their game. In the end, Dan remembered the tent poles, and we found them in the corner of the shed. Then we got on really well, because Dan's family goes camping, and he knows all about guy ropes and things, so he was the boss for that bit. There was a bit of a pause when we couldn't find any pegs for the ends of the string, but Imran said he'd seen them on the high-up shelf in the shed, and he was right.

After a long time, we got it all sorted out and it was really good. There was a way in where the brown sheet was, and a gap at the back for going out, and it was big enough for lots of children. We had two long bits of string to hold the sheets up, and *both tent poles, and lots of tent pegs and clothes pegs. When the teacher saw it, she looked really pleased. She said if we thought it was just right, hadn't we better draw a plan so we could make it again whenever we liked? So Lily rushed off to get a big piece of paper and some pens, and we put stickers on the poles and pegs, so when we put them in a special bag, we would be able to find them again.*

Lily's plan was just finished by picnic-time, and the teacher said it would be really useful; she stuck it up on the back of the shed door so everyone would know how to make the den from now on. After lunch, I went to help with the painting, but Lily, Dan and Imran played in the den right to the end when it was time to go home, and they really took turns and didn't wreck it in the end, like they do sometimes. After they'd put it all away I saw them standing in front of the plan, pointing at bits. They looked just like a gang of builders!

Children learn well with a combination of appropriately high expectations and appropriately high self-esteem

About expectations

This statement can be taken to refer to children's own expectations of themselves or to the expectations of their 'important adults'. Children's own expectations are comparatively straightforward to consider, if one is also engaged in considering their self-concept, as the one will inform the other. If children's self-concept is appropriately positive, then, correspondingly, their self-expectation is likely to be appropriately high.

The question of adults' expectations is more complex. Holding high expectations of children generally has a powerful effect on their learning (DES, 1989, pp. 31–4). If we accept that children need their 'important people's' acceptance and approval, it's not hard to see why this is. Children must meet those expectations – or at least be seen to try to do so – in order to retain the acceptance and approval that they need.

It is most important that our expectations of children grow out of our knowledge of their abilities, achievements and interests. Watching and listening to children must form the basis of our expectations of them; otherwise, there is a danger that children may become overwhelmed by inappropriately high expectations. When this happens, children may no longer feel able to explore, experiment and make 'safe' mistakes from which they can learn. They may cease to struggle for 'mastery' and become 'helpless'.

Some adults are so acutely aware of this pitfall, and of children's need for acceptance and approval, that their expectations are disastrously low. In addition, praise may be offered constantly and indiscriminately, rather than as a result of real effort and achievement. The likely result is that children are not challenged to develop real knowledge, understanding and skills; and, in addition, there is a danger that they will develop an inflated and unrealistic idea of their own ability and potential which becomes a major obstacle to their learning progress. Also, these children tend to be either insensitive to any sort of censure or extremely vulnerable to the slightest criticism. They do not have that inner core of self-confidence which enables them to accept criticism and use it positively.

Components of self-esteem

Some very general statements can usefully be made about self-esteem: what it is, what it does and how it develops. Firstly, high self-esteem – or positive self-concept – is reflected in the possession of a secure sense of identity, and an ability to acknowledge and value our own efforts and achievements. Secondly, high self-esteem provides confidence, energy and optimism. Thirdly, high self-esteem is promoted by positive self-experiences (Curry and Johnson, 1990). The way in which Lily, Dan and Imran tackled designing a den indicated high levels of self-esteem in those children. They knew what they wanted, and they went about the task with confidence, energy and optimism.

Self-esteem is a complex concept. The critical components ebb and flow at different stages of development, but nonetheless are life-long issues, with their roots in the early years. As already mentioned in Chapter 1, Curry and Johnson have described these components as control and power, competence, values, and acceptance. It is interesting to compare these components of self-esteem with the components of progression towards free-flow play, i.e. exploring, skills and competences, and ultimately the combination of competence with feelings and ideas. It would seem that there is much common ground between the development of free-flow play and the acquisition of high self-esteem. All four components of self-esteem are important; and, although one or other of three aspects – control and power, competence and value – may be dominant at different stages of a child's development, the fourth component – acceptance – appears to be crucial throughout.

Competition

Observations of babies, toddlers and young children reveal that they are predominantly concerned with gaining control, over themselves, over objects and over other people. Tiny babies struggle to control the movements of their hands and to lift up their heads; later, they spend hours on end investigating what happens when they drop, push or reach for. They engage in power-battles with parents, brothers and sisters, and their sense of self develops partly as a result of their success or failure with these things.

Later still, children begin to measure themselves, both in relation to their own knowledge and expectations of themselves, and in relation to each other. Some children become increasingly competitive, frequently comparing themselves with others. This then becomes the way that these children develop their sense of self-worth. Other children depend more on their own inner sense of power and control. These latter children have been helped to begin making judgements about their own achievements, to begin learning about directing their own behaviour, to begin managing the things they want to do, and to learn new knowledge and skills in collaboration with others. Lily, Dan and Imran's approach to den-making reflected this second approach.

There are disadvantages in encouraging children to compare themselves with others. Firstly, having winners necessitates having losers, and children who often experience not winning begin to see themselves as losers, and do not generally learn happily, confidently or competently – a downward spiral of decreasing self-confidence. Secondly, even the winners lose out. Such an approach only encourages them to be better than others; it does not expect or encourage a child's personal best, and more able children often learn to aim for lower than the summit.

It is often argued that competition is necessary, and so it is – in a way. But the most effective competition in the long term, and the sort that is most effective for *all* children, is the 'winners all' kind. This is when children are consistently engaged in winning against their own previous best, and in encouraging those around them to do the same.

Self-esteem and genuine praise

Self-esteem is related to our sense of our own significance and value. However, ideas about helping children to experience themselves as valuable and competent individuals have been open to misconception and trivialisation. For instance, the use of strategies such as habitual empty praise, gold stars, smiley stickers and meaningless statements, are more likely to feed children's self-preoccupation and narcissism than to help them form a genuine sense of their own worth (Docking, 1980).

Our responses to children have to be founded on realities if they are to carry meaning and avoid confusion and damage. This is one of the reasons why the recognition and acceptance of children's schemas can be such a useful and powerful way of looking at children. Genuine self-esteem in children comes from living with people who understand, accept and support them on the basis of reality.

How children learn to see themselves, right from the start, makes a profound impact on their approach to life in the long term. Concerns are sometimes expressed as to the value of early high self-esteem, suggesting that it can encourage children to be self-centred and selfish. These concerns are understandably a consequence of many children's responses to constant, automatic and undiscriminating praise. In Part 5 the case has been made for a very different kind of self-esteem: one resulting from a genuine recognition of children's *real* efforts and achievements. It has been argued here that children's awareness of their own efforts and achievements must be the realistic basis of their self-esteem, and of the inner confidence that underpins effective learning.

10

Adults aiming high

– AT THE BOTTOM OF THE DEEP BLUE SEA –

❛It was cold and wet all this week, and the day I went to nursery with Lily was the coldest and wettest. All the children stayed in, and lots of them were playing on the big hollow wooden blocks, making a boat.

Lily played with them for a while, but the children weren't really playing with each other. One boy was being really bossy and he was telling everyone what to do; he was doing all the best things himself, like being the driver. Lily soon got fed up and went off to do some painting. Some of the others stayed there a long time, though. The teacher helped them make a flag for the boat, and they had the steering wheel, and they got some paper plates and things out of the junk modelling box and had a pretend picnic.

There's always a group-time every day, when the children talk about things with the teacher and have songs and stories. Most of the children at Lily's group-time had been pretending in the boat, but the bossy boy wasn't there. One of the girls had made a little puppet on a lolly stick, and it had yellow wool for its hair. When she saw the puppet, Lily's teacher said it reminded her of something, and when they'd finished their milk and sung the song about the bottom of the deep, blue sea and it was story-time, she said it was like something that has long fair hair and a fish's tail instead of legs! The children all knew she meant a mermaid, and then she said she was going to tell them a story about a family of sailors, and there was a mermaid in the story, too.

The teacher must have made up the story as she went along, because it was bit like when the children were pretending. Right at the beginning, as soon as she said something about the sailors having a picnic, Dan said, 'You're thinking about our one!' and he was really pleased.

When they came to the picnic bit of the story, the teacher asked them what they thought sailors like to eat. Lily said, 'Fish', quite loudly but Dan said, 'Worms', even louder. The teacher laughed at Dan's worms and she made the sailors in the story take their spades and tramp off to the fields to dig up worms for their picnic and put them in a little pot. That made Dan really pleased with his idea, and the children thought it was funny. Then the teacher made a pretend fishing rod by tying a piece of string to the end of a stick, and she made the sailor in the story catch the mermaid by mistake.

When the sailors were wondering whether she'd be good to eat, I thought Lily's and Aisha's eyes would fall out of their heads, they were listening so hard. But the teacher made one of the sailors notice that she was frightened and be friends with her, so they decided to catch some proper fish instead, and she was safe.

In the story all sorts of things happened; the teacher showed them how to make lots of paper fishes at once, by folding the paper before you cut the fish shape, and the sailors had an argument about how many fishes they had caught, so they had to count them lots of times. The teacher made a pretend bonfire with some little sticks from the bush outside, and in the story they swam to a desert island and made a special shelter for sleeping. Then they took it in turns to look after each other by keeping a lookout for wild animals, and then they had to agree about what to have for breakfast. In the story, one of the sailors wanted to go home to his mum, and all the others made sure he was all right until the aeroplane came to rescue them.

Some days, the teacher makes up stories, and some days she just tells them or reads them from books. After the sailor story nearly all of the children wanted to go straight back to the blocks, and it was really interesting. Their pretending was different – much more with each other than before, pretending and making things that had been in the story and making up new things as well, like a monster that came out of the sea.

After a little while, the bossy boy came back again, and I thought he might spoil it. Amy was doing the steering, and the boy tried to push her out of the way. I was just going to stop him, when she looked him right in the eye and said, 'It's my turn'. The boy looked at her and looked at the wheel and the other children watching, and he didn't say anything, he just went off and joined the picnic! I saw the teacher give him a big smile, so she must have been pleased with him for doing that. ❜

Children are encouraged to learn when someone knows what they especially want to do and can nearly manage, and helps them to manage it successfully

Ways of helping children's learning

How children learn and *what* they learn go hand in hand. Two strategies can help to achieve this balance of how and what. First, we can look for ways in which we can identify, support and extend those things that children *want* to do, and having an understanding of schemas helps with this (Athey, 1990). Second, we can look for ways to identify, support and extend those things that children can *nearly* do (Vygotsky, 1978). Here, adults can help by having an understanding of the development of children's self-esteem, with its components of acceptance, power and control, competence, and values (Curry and Johnson, 1990).

Children feel empowered to struggle with what they can nearly do when they know they are accepted, when they feel a sense of power and control, when they have sufficient competence, and when their efforts are valued. Our role as supporting adults can include watching and listening, questioning, accepting and encouraging, giving help when it is genuinely needed, enabling and encouraging reflection and planning, and recognising, valuing and applauding only *real* efforts and achievements.

The teacher's watching and listening was helpful because of the ideas she was able to give the children as a result. She had observed their interests and the level at which they would be likely to operate. Her interest and encouragement during the group-time helped them to talk to each other and to her about what had happened and what they wanted to do. Once they had the ideas, the addition of a blanket here and a few sticks there was enough for them to get on. The children needed something to pretend with, but nothing complicated.

Using puppets, either home-made or bought, can be a good way of introducing issues and ideas in a neutral way. If the puppet has been made by a child, as the mermaid puppet was, using it in this way can be particularly effective for children.

Lily's teacher had watched the children pretending and had noticed what they wanted to do and some of the problems they were having. Their needs had included a few props and some ways of dealing with situations. She fulfilled these needs, and once she had given them some ideas and suggestions, the children could continue to elaborate for themselves. They used her support, and took her ideas further.

The teacher's watching and listening served another purpose. Without being inhibited by it, the children were conscious of her attention and were supported by that. Sometimes this 'containing' function can be provided by a more able child. Vygotsky (1978, p. 87) describes children solving problems with adults' – or more able peers' – assistance. This is not the sort of helping where we do the difficult things *for* children, sometimes suggesting that, if they watch, one day they will be able to do it. The essence of this other sort of help is that the learners are the 'doers', while the supporters watch, *with appropriate optimism*. This appropriate optimism is the key to the process; it is the supporter's (realistic) confidence in the learner's ability that can affect the learner's self-expectation and enable the learner to break new ground.

– FRIDAY NIGHTS AT HOME –

❝ *Everybody's always in on Friday nights – the first part of Friday nights, anyway. The kids' dad really minds about it. He says it's important that everybody can talk about things and that we all listen to each other. That's why we all have our meal together on Fridays; Mum says it's the only time she knows we're all going to see each other, and sometimes she cooks special things, if she hasn't been too busy.*

I wouldn't miss it, anyway. There's Mum, the kids' dad, Lily, Joe and me. Sometimes there's a grown-up friend of Mum's or their dad's as well, but Mum and their dad don't talk to their friends instead of us; everybody joins in together. I like listening to everybody talking and I like watching Joe, too. Last Friday, he had his drink out of a glass for the first time, just like the rest of us; everybody cheered, and he was really proud of himself.

We had a big discussion that evening about when Lily pretended sailors at the nursery – Lily said it was her favourite, and told them all about it. I said, 'What about when you played moving house with Henna?' And Lily said that was her favourite, too. Then Mum said weren't they both about the same thing, really about taking things from one place to another? Lily said, 'I like doing it,' and Mum said, 'I know,' and smiled at her. Then Lily said, 'Henna likes boxes – and the shopping basket.' And Mum said, 'We'll have to give her the bag to carry when she comes to the seaside with us next week.'

Then we all talked about what going to the seaside would be like, and what we wanted to do. Lily said she wanted to take her dolls in their buggy, and Mum said couldn't we take them without the buggy and Lily said, 'No!' very loudly. Her dad said he hoped they'd still have the coconut shy on the pier and the rifle range. Mum said she couldn't understand why he liked those things, and she was going to look for that wonderful machine that makes fresh doughnuts with lots of jam in the middle. They asked me next, and I said I like those train things that go up and down, and Lily said, 'That's at the fair,' and Joe jigged up and down and said, 'Train, train.' Then Mum grinned at him and said, 'We'll just take the Duplo, that'll keep you happy'. Joe looked anxious, so she said, 'Ice-cream?' and he jigged again.

Then the kids' dad said that he'd heard Lily's teacher talking about the way some children specially like doing the same sort of thing a lot of the time and that it's about patterns and the way children think about things. 'You and Lily's Henna think about things inside other things,' he said to Mum, 'and I like throwing and shooting and kicking footballs, all about moving lines.' They started arguing about whether he liked those things specially because he's a dad, but then they both laughed.

After that, it was time for pudding, and they laughed again because Mum had made her favourite, which is apple pasties with sultanas inside. Dad said he'd just remembered Lily's teacher saying that some children like taking things from one place to another and that must be the pattern that Lily has. Then I thought that when it's Lily's birthday next week, I'll give her the little rucksack I saw in the luggage-shop window, and then she can collect stones and things on the beach and bring them back safely. If Henna comes with us, perhaps I'd better get one for her too; she'd love putting things in it, and then they can carry their own treasures, all the way home.

'Talk about my day,' Lily said in bed that night. She always says that at bed-time, and you have to start with when she got up and go through everything that's happened. Sometimes you can skip bits, or she interrupts with things you didn't know. She really likes the naughty bits – and the times when people have been pleased with her. She likes talking about when she was upset, too, like the time Dan wasn't her friend any more because she'd had the best bike. Talking about it seems to make her feel better. Last Friday, she told me all about her new friend at school, Nicholas, who has a special wheelchair and looks funny. Lily says the other children don't play with him much, but the other day he let her put all her things on his lap so she could take them

outside, and now he's her friend. And last Friday she wasn't going to go to sleep until she'd told me all over again about what she and Henna are going to do at the seaside! **>**

Recognising and supporting the development of children's patterns of learning, or schemas, leads to high self-esteem

Using schemas

Everybody needs the feeling that they are accepted, understood and valued. The recognition and acceptance by adults of children's schematic patterns contributes to these feelings in children. Schemas are at the heart of children's individuality, and so to recognise and support them appropriately is to recognise and support the child on a very fundamental level.

Using our knowledge of schemas can also make it much easier to help children develop skills and competence. Dan's hand–eye co-ordination will improve if we give him the new set of skittles, because his particular schema is a 'trajectory' one. Jessica's hand–eye co-ordination needs improvement too, but she is unlikely to show much interest in skittles. The way to encourage her to concentrate on hand–eye co-ordination for long enough to show a significant improvement, is to introduce her to the new construction set, possibly asking her to check that all the pieces fit together. She is likely to tackle this with concentration and persistence, because her schema is concerned with connecting.

Children planning and reflecting

Thinking and talking about what is *going* to happen is an important stage in the cycle of learning. There is now a growing emphasis among teachers on ways in which children can be more closely involved in the planning of their work; and everyone who makes a practice of this involvement will be in no doubt about its value (Lally, 1991, p. 69). Lily's appreciation of her day at the seaside, and her use of time on that day, will have been sharpened by the family discussion at tea the Friday before. This sort of approach, helping children to 'look ahead', is instrumental in nurturing a 'mastery' approach to learning, rather than a 'helpless' approach.

Less recognised, as yet, is the value of reflection with children. On a very ordinary level, it can be seen that occasions for talking over children's successful experiences with them are likely to raise their confidence, optimism and self-esteem. In addition, to be supported and encouraged in thinking and talking about unsuccessful or painful experiences means that children are much more likely to be able to learn from them positively.

The pressures of modern living and teaching make it increasingly difficult to pause to reflect with children. There seems always to be too much to do and too little time. In schools, it is common to see lessons which end with clearing up after the practical work is finished, and the time for important discussion about the children's experiences is missed (Driver, 1983). Activity by itself is not enough; it is the sense that is made of activity that matters.

Bed-time is often a good time for looking back over things. The next day is probably too late, and it's often hard to think about how and why something happened while still angry, hurt or elated. Bed-time offers enough detachment, but not too much; it also offers security. Children tend to feel comparatively secure at bed-time, possibly because the time, the place and the people are usually the same. Honest reflection does require an element of security. We all need to feel safe to think about mistakes, to feel proud of successes and to make useful connections between what has happened and what we will do next.

It is harder for staff to establish such a sense of security in a school setting, but the same principles can be made to apply – same times, same places, same people. This can represent quite a challenge in terms of organisation and management, but it is one worth tackling. We need to look for ways of establishing opportunities for reflection and planning. Does our organisation lend itself to this sort of provision? Do we already have situations which could, with a little adjustment, be used in this way? What about, for instance, an approach to school meals which encourages and enables conversation and discussion?

Regular opportunities to review and discuss past experiences, and to look forward together with others to new ones, are of great value. They can make a world of difference to such factors as children's aspirations, motivation, socialisation and self-esteem. It is these factors that are claimed to be the most important learning in pre-school education (Ball, 1994, p. 22).

Eating together

We recognise that 'doing' is an important part of the learning process. Time for play, when children are 'doing' at their highest level, is quality time for children. But time spent in looking backwards and forwards is quality time too. This is no less true at home than at school, where all too often the pace and pressure of life means that we see very little of our families in situations where we can make the most of being together. How can families make sure, for the sake both of adults and of children, that they have regular 'quality time' together?

One answer – Lily's dad's answer – is regular family meals. For some families, this means every day, and they are fortunate if the pattern of all their lives makes this practical. For others, it is harder; maybe working hours are variable, or perhaps someone – the baby or the adult on a night shift – is always asleep. These sorts of problems may result in less frequent family meals. There is no doubt that, for many families, eating together regularly presents real problems; but it's worth trying to get around the problems at least sometimes, so that families have a time when everyone can talk about their day (like Lily), and maybe share their feelings, hopes and plans.

Many adults – and indeed many older children – say that their experiences of eating together have not produced these benefits; that on the contrary, family meals tend to result in misunderstandings, stress and indigestion. Perhaps, for them, meals have not been thought of as times for listening, affirming, supporting and discussing, as well as eating. There are other factors, too, that get in the way of family meals. Often it isn't that families have decided not to eat together, but that other things just seem to happen. Maybe it's someone's favourite television programme, or perhaps the children are in bed. Alternatively, perhaps the children are not in bed, but we wish they were, so we feed them quickly and get firm about bed-time. Sometimes houses don't seem to be designed with family meals in mind; there isn't enough space for everyone to sit down together, or the only big table is needed for other things. But 'where there's a will there's a way' – and it may be worth it, in more ways than have been realised. One US survey of 4,756 middle and high school students, reported in *Eating Well* magazine in June 2005, showed that children who sat down to meals most often with their families (seven or more times a week) tended to have higher grade point averages and were more well adjusted. They were also less likely to feel depressed, to smoke or use alcohol; and this was found to be the case even after race, family structure and social class had been taken into account. So maybe there needs to be some discussion, among the older people in the family at least, about the possibilities, pleasures and advantages of eating together.

– FUN AND FIREWORKS –

❛ It's nearly the summer holidays, and last week was the nursery picnic. It's a good thing there's quite a bit of space outside at that nursery because lots of families were there, and all the teachers and their families, and even some 'old' families from other years. It was a really warm evening, and there were loads of children and babies – all the nursery ones, and brothers and sisters, too.

I helped to get things ready, but there wasn't much to do after the nursery was tidied up at the end of the afternoon. We took all the tables outside and put them end to end with pretty paper on them; and we blew up lots of balloons and hung them on the posts and pillars and on the branches of the tree. Henna and Imran's mums had been cooking with the children in the afternoon, making samosas, and we put those on plates and got the orange squash ready. Fatima's dad brought two round tarts that he'd made for the picnic, and Lily and me cut them up into equal pieces. After that, people started to come, and they all brought things for everybody to eat. We put the *food out on the long table on nursery plates, so everybody could help themselves.*

Mum and Joe arrived; Mum had brought the salad that we'd made last night and a blanket for us to sit on. Lily gave Joe a big hug and took him off to play with her friends in their camp. That was the last we saw of them for ages, and when their dad came later, nearly all the food was gone, but Mum had saved him some. He brought his friends Andy and Steve; Andy had what Mum calls his squeeze-box with him, for play-ing dancing music, and Steve had his fiddle. When Lily saw it, she rushed off to get her friends, and when he started playing, they held hands and jumped about pretending to dance; and people stood around in a circle and clapped.

After a while, Lily's teacher asked Andy if we could do a proper dance, and Andy said he and Steve could play one if someone would stand in the middle and teach people what to do. Mum's friend Wendy said she knew some dances and that she'd help. We had to have partners; some people joined in, and some just wanted to watch. I was going to watch, but the kids' dad said I was his partner and Mum was with Dan's mum, and everybody got in a muddle and laughed a lot. Soon, Wendy said she knew we could do it properly, and then we did, and it was really fun. After that, we got lots of children to come and dance as well, and that was the best part. We just did the easy bits and the going round and round bits, and the children loved it. I had Joe, and Mum had Lily. Joe could only go round and round with me hanging on to him tight, but he really loved the music and the jigging about.

When Andy was putting his squeeze-box away he said if we liked, he could give us a tape of the music. Then when the children had got really good at going up and down and round and round, we could decide what order we wanted to do it in and make up our own nursery dance. Lily's teacher thought that was a great idea; she said it would be really good to know how to do some dances properly. And it would be even more fun, once we knew how to do them well enough, to play around with the dances and make our own.

It was nearly dark by the time everyone had finished eating and dancing and chat-ting and playing, and some of the babies were asleep. Lily and Joe were wide awake, though. We were just thinking about going home, when everyone had a lovely surprise. One of the teachers (not Lily's) was leaving the nursery because her family was mov-ing, and she had brought some fireworks for a special treat, to say goodbye to every-one. There were Roman Candles and Silver Rain and Catherine Wheels; and this teacher had made sure that the fireworks had no really loud bangs, so nobody was frightened. The last one was a really amazing rocket; it whooshed up with a sort of swishing noise and covered the sky with tiny little gold and silver stars that floated away gently in the dark. **9**

Children learn well with a combination of appropriately high expectations and appropriately high self-esteem

Self-esteem in early childhood education and care settings

In schools and early years settings, there are a number of practical strategies that are relevant to the ways in which children learn to see themselves. It can be illuminating to ask ourselves some questions, for instance about organisation, adults' approaches, and assessment and recording arrangements. Are there times for all the children to listen and be heard, about how they feel and what they have done? Do all the children have opportunities to make genuine choices? How much are all children trusted and given responsibility?

In relation to adults, are staff aware of their priorities? Do they give clear messages about those priorities to children and parents? Do children have an 'important person'? What is that person's role and responsibility? What behaviour management strategies are there? What support is there for children as they move to their next school? Are these strategies and arrangements consistent with developing positive self-concept in children?

Assessment and recording arrangements carry a world of hidden messages for children and parents. Is a positive model used, one which identifies children's special strengths as well as areas for support? Is there accurate and detailed information about children? Do adults make sure that children share their successes, both with their parents and with each other?

These questions raise some of the issues which have a direct bearing on how children learn to see themselves, and which make a major impact on children's learning dispositions. More about dispositions is to be found in Part 6. Attention to these sorts of details may have a profound effect on children's approach to learning. Our attention to them is surely the entitlement of every child.

Working together

From birth onwards, an increasing variety of people will be involved with each child. As well as the usual widening circle of family and friends, there will be those involved in the child's health, welfare and education. Parents are generally the most, and sometimes the only, permanent players in this shifting cast of adults. Increasingly, this is being recognised and used positively by those who work with young children, for instance in the use of parent-held child health and development records.

Continuity and co-ordination between all the people who work with children is crucially important (David, 1990, p. 153). Unless we have an awareness of the unseen pieces in the jigsaw of a child's life, we may not be especially effective, helpful or reassuring to that child. This is particularly important for the many children who are meeting adults from different cultures than their own and for children with special needs. All children need continuity and co-ordination; but the more adults there are involved with a child, and the more diverse they are, the more important this becomes. At all levels, we need to be working towards a more coherent experience for young children and their families.

Freedom and responsibility

Much of this book is about achieving a balance in situations that affect us all. It is about how feelings affect learning, and how learning affects feelings; about meeting individual needs within the wider context of the family and society, and about considering the needs of others without losing sight of the individual; about the way in which our responses to children affect their development, and how their development dictates our responses to them.

It has been argued that satisfying learning experiences in early childhood result in children who want to learn and who see the point in struggling to do so. Teachers of older children, as well as parents and employers, will certainly testify to the extreme importance of developing these positive learning dispositions, in which children understand the value of learning in terms of usefulness and pleasure.

There has been considerable emphasis on children's need for understanding and for freedom to 'be themselves'. However, Chapters 5 and 6 also stress the importance of children's perceptions of themselves, not only as individuals, but also as part of a larger group – of the family, the community, our multi-cultural society, ultimately of all humanity. At the heart of this balance between the needs of the individual and society lie the issues of responsibility and freedom. To be given total responsibility and no freedom seriously inhibits children's ability to develop and to learn, and would rarely now be advocated. Complete freedom, together with few or no expectations of responsibility, is a more frequent state of affairs, but unfortunately the price tends to be unhappy, anarchic children now, and disaffected, anti-social adults to come.

Children do need freedom. But not total freedom, which lacks the security of containment, the reassurance of limits, the way towards self-control. Our greatest challenge is to try to achieve for children an appropriate combination of freedom and responsibility. This is how to make the most of early learning – and how to be ready, willing and able for school, and ready, willing and able for life.

POSTSCRIPT TO PART 5: REAL SELF-ESTEEM

Living or working with young children?
Questions to think about . . .

> ### Children are encouraged to learn when someone knows what they especially want to do and can nearly manage, and helps them to manage it successfully

1. What strategies and theories can we use in order to discover what children especially want to do, and can nearly manage?

> ### Recognising and supporting the development of children's patterns of learning, or schemas, leads to high self-esteem

2. How can we recognise and support the development of children's schemas?

> ### Children learn well with a combination of appropriately high expectations and appropriately high self-esteem

3. What can be done by important adults to support the development of appropriately high self-esteem in young children?

RECOMMENDED FURTHER READING

For sharing with children . . .

Browne, E. (1994), *Handa's Surprise*, London, Walker Books

This lovely book is both a joke, and a story about friendship and generosity. Handa chooses seven delicious fruits and puts them in a basket to carry on her head to her friend Akeyo who lives in another village. But why are there eight fruits in the enchanting end papers, and eight animals too? The text is beautifully simple, and the illustrations superb.

Hughes, S. (1993), *Giving*, London, Walker Books

Here is another book about generosity, and with lovely end papers too; young children spend hours poring over these and weaving new stories around the little characters. This is about everyday life for young children, and how we give each other things all the time as well as presents on special occasions . . . kisses and hugs, slices of apple and soggy crusts, cross looks or big smiles.

. . . and for a good read

Paley, V.G. (2004), *A Child's Work: The Importance of Fantasy Play*, Chicago, IL, Chicago University Press

Vivian Paley writes about 'the intensity and intentionality' of very young children playing – the only age group 'that is always busy making up its own work assignments'. We see fascinating and vital vignettes of play and creativity – vignettes that persuasively convince us of the critical role of fantasy play in the psychological, intellectual and social development of young children. This remarkable book is wonderfully readable, and very hard to put down once you have started – except that you do want to put it down occasionally, to give yourself a chance to think about it.

PART 6

NEW JOURNEYS

11

Children managing transitions

– LISA COMES TO STAY –

❛ The day after the picnic at Lily's nursery, Lisa came to stay. Mum says she's a sort of cousin, something to do with Mum's family. Lisa's two years older than me and goes to College, and she's come to see Lily and Joe. She says she has to watch them for her college work, and find out about the big school that Lily's going to next now she's too big for Nursery, because her project is called 'Transitions'. She wants to come with us when we do things. Mum says I should talk to Lisa about Lily and Joe because I know so much about them now – not so much as her though, but when I said that she said she was too busy to talk to Lisa much. I'm pleased she thinks I can do it instead of her. Anyway, Lisa's cool.

But Joe isn't sure about Lisa yet. Last night at bed-time Lily and Joe talked through their day as usual – they love that – only Joe was a bit shy until I helped him. Then we were having bed-time stories, and it was Joe's turn to choose. When he picked out the same old 'Where's the Bear?' story again we all groaned, but he really wanted it, and then he had to have it three times! So it took quite a long time, and when it was Lily's turn to tell it she kept skipping a page, and every time Joe screamed at her. She was teasing him, making him scream on purpose, especially when she started leaving out the song. I had to promise we'd play the game about it tomorrow, to calm him down.

I think Joe likes Lisa though. She smiles at him and she's always interested in what he does, and he likes that. Lisa was really surprised that he still wanted that story when he knew it by heart already – and that he really knows about books when he's so small. But Lily told her that Joe's always had books and stories, since the day he was born.

Lisa knows about big schools already because they told her at College, and she went on visits with the other students. She says she wants to know how Lily feels about going to Big School, and what she knows about it, and how she found out. Lily really likes it when people want to know what she thinks so I'm sure she'll tell Lisa lots of things, and I'm going to listen too. ❜

Children in transition need to know what to expect, with *time* and *support* to reflect on their experiences and to look forward to new ones; and *confidence* that adults will understand and respect their needs

Part 6 follows the previous two-chapter pattern: the first chapter is about the children themselves, while the second chapter focuses mainly on adults who live and work with the youngest children.

Transitions

The final part of this book focuses on transitions – those shifts that all babies and young children make sooner or later: from one person to another, from place to place, from one group of friends to the next. These can be traumatic times for very young children, and yet with understanding by adults right from the start there is much that can be done to make transitions smooth and even positive experiences.

The most acknowledged and often challenging transition for many children and their families is the one from home to school, and so this is the main focus of these final chapters. Hilary Fabian (in Dunlop and Fabian, 2002) discusses the ways in which children can be empowered for transition into the culture of the school, pointing out that there will be a complex process for both school and child; with the school adjusting to the needs of the child, and the child learning about the needs of the culture. She highlights four attributes of resilient children: social competence, problem-solving skills, autonomy, and a sense of purpose and future; and makes a strong case for using stories in a variety of practical ways to help children through transitions.

Effectively, issues relating to transition generally are likely to arise when a child first attends a child-minder or a day-care setting, or perhaps at about three years in a nursery class which is an integrated part of a primary school. There are many possible situations which result in young children being somewhere on a continuum from home to school; however the moment on which these two chapters focus is when a child begins to spend all day at school, probably at age 4 to 5. This time constitutes more of a new start for some than others; at the one end of the spectrum will be children who have become used to life with other children and adults, possibly in a day nursery or Children's Centre; and who already know the school building well, and maybe also the teachers and many of the conventions too. This is often the case where a 'transition' child has an older sibling already at the school. At the other end of the spectrum are children who have spent the years from birth at home, with little or no group experience; and for whom starting at primary school will be a completely new experience in every respect.

'Properly' being four

What does it feel like to be a child 'on the move'? How do children manage? Early childhood is full of transitions: from womb to world, from cradle to cot, from one person to another, from one place to another. Successfully managing early transitions can generate a bedrock of stability for later 'life event' ones. A particular focus of this book has been the ways in which babies and young children can manage the normal transitions of early childhood in ways that will help to build their longer-term emotional health and well-being. These last two chapters draw this thinking together, examining some of the issues arising for children and for the adults who live and work with them, in transitions from home to school.

In no sense, though, is the whole purpose of early childhood from birth seen as a preparation for later challenges on entry to school. This book aims to show how vital it is that we acknowledge and support experiences in the earliest years *for their own sake*. Early childhood is a crucially important time, not as a preparation for later life but in its own right. And the very best preparation for being five lies in *properly* being four, three, two and one. Gopnik *et al.* (1999, p. 201) put it like this:

> One benefit of knowing the science is a kind of protective scepticism. It should make us deeply suspicious of any enterprise that offers a formula for making babies smarter or teaching them more, from flash cards to Better Baby Institutes. Everything we know about babies suggests that these artificial interventions are at best useless, and at worst distractions from the normal interaction between grown-ups and babies. Babies are already as smart as they can be, they know what they need to know, and they are very effective and selective in getting the kinds of information they need. They are designed to learn about the real world that surrounds them, and they learn by playing with the things in that world, most of all by playing with the people that love them.

However, these final chapters on transition draw on the thinking of the rest of the book. In doing so they identify some of the many ways in which relationships and play, which do so much to make the most of early childhood for its own sake, can in fact lay down the foundations for later self-esteem and learning throughout life.

A holistic view of children

How we support children in transition – moving from one situation to another – depends very much on how we think of those children. How *do* we view babies and young children? Perhaps as little empty jugs, gradually being filled up with knowledge? Or do we see babies and young children as possessing astonishing knowledge, skills and understanding for their years – a concept of 'half full' rather than 'half empty'? Sensitive adults living with and caring for young children down the centuries have been surprised and delighted by their use of language, newly acquired skills and fresh view of the world. But it is only recently, as the imaging techniques of neuroscience begin to map the early development of the brain, that a more universal awareness of the competence and the potential of very young children is beginning to emerge.

Now we know that the way very young children learn about the physical world is by exploring, playing and observing the relations between objects, with people who love them and know them well. Tiny babies learn about other people, naturally imitating their gestures, facial expressions and actions (Trevarthen and Aitken, 2001). They can tell the difference between facial expressions of happiness, sadness and anger, and their ability to understand other people's emotions continues to develop throughout the first few years of life. It seems that they begin to develop a 'theory of mind' at the age of about four, starting to realise not only that they believe certain things (e.g. I *think* Joe's book is in his room) but that people can have different beliefs from their own, and that they themselves can have different beliefs at different times (Blakemore, 2000). Children learn mainly through their own experiences of playing, exploring, everyday conversations and generally being with other people.

One of the most influential approaches to children's learning since the 1960s has been the provision for children under six years in Reggio Emilia in Northern Italy. The 'Reggio approach' has gained world-wide recognition for its inspirationally profound view of children as strong, powerful and competent learners; and its emphasis on community and citizenship. The founder of the Reggio approach to early education, Loris Malaguzzi wrote:

> Our image of children no longer considers them as isolated and egocentric, does not only see them as engaged in action with objects, does not emphasise only the cognitive aspects, does not belittle feelings or what is not logical and does not consider with ambiguity the role of the reflective domain. Instead our image of the child is rich in potential, strong, powerful, competent and most of all connected to adults and children. (Malaguzzi, in Penn, 1997, p. 117)

Here Malaguzzi, an early years educator, highlights the need to think beyond cognition to a more holistic view of the child. In 1996, only the year before, the New Zealand Early Childhood Curriculum 'Te Whariki' was published. The following aspirations for children on which 'Te Whariki' is founded reveal how coherent was the thinking in Northern Italy and New Zealand at around the same time:

> To grow up as competent and confident learners and communicators, healthy in mind, body and spirit, secure in their sense of belonging and in the knowledge that they make a valued contribution to society. (New Zealand Ministry of Education, 1996, p. 9)

These more holistic and challenging approaches acknowledge the impact of all aspects of children's development on each other, so that as well as thinking about emotional, social, cognitive and physical development as separate strands we learn to weave them together and look at the whole picture.

Margaret Carr (2001) in New Zealand suggests the importance of 'foregrounding' and 'backgrounding' aspects of children's development, emphasising the need as we foreground (or prioritise) less familiar aspects of child development, not to lose sight of other more familiar aspects. We sometimes need to foreground emotional development, for instance, but never over-looking the concurrent learning and social development in the background. This holistic thinking about child development is reflected in the structure of this book, in which each section foregrounds a different aspect, while using the narratives to retain in the background of our focused thinking the holistic view of the child that is so essential.

Attributes that help children manage transitions

In a training resource developed for the National Children's Bureau, Bird and Gerlach (2005, p. 6) describe essential emotional health and well-being as:

> . . . the subjective capacity and state of mind that supports us to feel good about how we are and confident to deal with present and future circumstances. It is influenced by our emotional development and how resilient and resourceful we feel ourselves to be.

The authors propose eleven attributes as important for 'good enough' emotional health and wellbeing, as follows: 1. A secure sense of who you are; 2. A sense of being able to be yourself; 3. A sense of belonging to a few significant people; 4. A sense of self-worth; 5. A belief in your own ability to influence things and make changes; 6. An ability to identify, ask for and move towards things you need; 7. An ability to recognise, care about and take responsibility for the impact of your behaviour on others; 8. Willing and able to do things with others and /or alone; 9. A capacity to tolerate uncertainty, and respond creatively and with integrity to challenges; 10. A capacity to respect the need for boundaries; and 11. A way of making sense of their experiences.

Adult readers will be able to identify with these attributes, but how do they work for young children, and how do young children develop them? In the table on the following page, each attribute is linked to one of the illustrative narratives in earlier chapters, with its following text. The narratives show how the foundations of these emotional health and wellbeing attributes lie in the very early situations and experiences described in this book.

ATTRIBUTES	NARRATIVES	PAGE NO.
1 A secure sense of who you are	FRIDAY NIGHTS AT HOME	116
2 A sense of being able to be yourself	PRETEND PAINTING	93
3 A sense of belonging to a few significant people	INTRODUCING JOE	3
4 A sense of self-worth	DAD'S HOME!	17
5 A belief in your own ability to influence things and make changes	BUILDING A DEN	108
6 An ability to identify, ask for and move towards things you need	LILY NEEDS HER DOLLS	51
7 An ability to recognise, care about and take responsibility for the impact of your behaviour on others	DAN STAYS THE NIGHT	69
8 Willing and able to do things with others and/or alone	JOE AT NURSERY	91
9 A capacity to tolerate uncertainty, and respond creatively and with integrity to challenges	LILY'S SUPERMAN	22
10 A capacity to respect the need for boundaries	EATING CUSTARD CREAMS	64
11 A way of making sense of their experiences	SHOPPING WITH DAD	57

So what *kinds* of situations and experiences help the development of these attributes, especially for children in transition? Four aspects are central here: a holistic view of children; their need for continuity and consistency; their need for time and support; and the importance of 'learning dispositions'. The first three are considered in this section, with 'Going to Big School' as a key transition in early childhood. 'Learning dispositions' are the focus of the final section in this chapter.

Children's need for continuity and consistency

Two often implicit but recurring threads running through this book have been about continuity, and consistency; and these are the threads that by their very nature will be stretched and sometimes snapped in times of transition. Nevertheless, continuity – the *continuum* of the journey – can be maintained in periods of transition. At any given moment, the threads of our journeys are many and varied, like a multi-coloured skein of silk. With all the threads intact, the skein is quite strong. With a few broken it will be less strong but still functional. We need to know, when some of the threads are broken, that the remainingones will still work for us; and this is especially the case for children.

In transitions, familiar people, things, places and routines become even more important then usual, and the more they can be maintained through periods of transition, the better. The week when a family moves house will definitely not be the time to buy the new cot, or leave the familiar old high-chair behind and start on 'grown-up' chairs. The month when a child moves from one day-care room to another will not be the time to make new arrangements for taking and collecting at the nursery. The arrival of a new baby or the loss of a much-loved member of the family will be a time to try and stick to established routines and familiarity, rather than look for distractions. Children need continuity, in order to manage change.

Something else that children need at such times is consistency from their important people, and between those people. This has been discussed in Chapter 6 in the context of thinking about 'unreasonable' behaviour; and also in Chapter 10 in the context of 'the unseen pieces in the jigsaw of a child's life'. But in terms of managing transitions, consistency takes on an added importance. 'Say yes as often as you can, and when you say no, mean it' is a helpful factor here. Moving from one situation to another means that while some new doors open, other doors close. This can be painful, and so while children are managing these transitions it is especially important to them that people say 'yes' as often as they can. And when a child is hoping for a 'yes' and gets a 'no', at such times it can feel especially trying. Sometimes it is possible for the adult to say 'no' in a different way, turning it into a 'yes': for instance, 'that piece of paper is for Lily, but here's one that is just right for you, would you like to paint on this one?' Saving the outright 'no's for the kinds of things that incontrovertibly matter (running across the road without looking, biting the baby, etc.), and making sure that everyone around the child agrees on what those things are, can be really helpful to the child.

When young children first experience a move from home to a situation involving a different primary carer (such as a child-minder, or a key worker in a day-care setting) it is essential that as much information as possible is shared between the primary carers. Doing this means that continuity and consistency are much more likely to be maintained, and this will help the child to manage the transition smoothly. The best way to do this is by spending time together with the child, talking together, and planning for eventualities. Probably the most helpful thing of all is for the baby or young child to feel that the two adults involved not only like him or her but that they like and respect each other. This sense of solidarity between the carers is extremely important for the child's sense of security, and is something that cannot really be 'faked' for the sake of the child, but needs to be genuinely achieved. Undoubtedly a little time invested at this stage will pay enormous dividends for everyone in the future.

And when young children move from one setting to another, usually some form of written information is passed from one setting to the next. This can be enormously useful in terms of continuity and consistency, provided it is valued and made use of – although it must be said that while a written record can be enormously important and helpful, it is no substitute for real conversations – especially ones in which the child also plays a part.

Children's need for time and support

Times of change tend to be busy times, especially for adults. This can be when usual routines of time spent together may be suspended, especially when all the busy-ness seems to be for the sake of the child, and their time has definitely been used up! But these are the very situations that generate uncertainty for children, when they are not sure what to expect and often worry about what will happen and whether they will be able to manage. At times of change it is important for children to be able to talk about what is happening, and to be able to ask questions about what is going to happen. Making the time and space for these conversations between children and parents or carers can be difficult, but is enormously important.

Such conversations can be very hard for very young children who are still learning how to say what they feel and think; and indeed adults are sometimes not very good at it either! Young children may not have the ability to explain how they feel in ways that we can easily understand. It will need all the skill and patience we can muster. One problem is that it is hard for children to 'save' their worries for an 'appropriate' moment and so a conversation that might have been comparatively straightforward at bed-time is much harder to manage sensitively on the way home from school in a hurry. While we can only do the best we can when the time comes, it is certainly helpful for children to become used to relating things that have happened, in ways that include how they feel and what they think. This is what Joe and Lily were doing as they 'talked through their day as usual'; such a routine, that has been happening for as long as a child can remember, helps enormously at times of transition or difficulty.

The ways in which children have experienced previous changes are all part of the picture. They need the confidence that their important adults will listen carefully to them, and will treat their needs with understanding and respect. There are so many opportunities for helping this confidence to develop over the years from birth, both at home and in day-care – minor opportunities like learning to sleep in a big bed or enjoying a new playground in the park; and major ones like moving house, a new sibling, or getting to know a new key person in day-care. The ways in which adults support babies and young children through these experiences profoundly affect children's confidence as they approach subsequent transitions. Reassurance, explanations, careful listening, praise, love and affection all will help babies and young children to develop the confidence they will need.

Going to Big School

For teachers everywhere, the first few days of the school year feel different – in spite of the challenge of 'gearing up', almost magic. In every primary school, a few (or maybe many) excited and/or apprehensive children are arriving for the first time: with bags carefully packed, new school clothes and eyes shining, sometimes eager, sometimes shy, what are their expectations? What will the first few days be like for them? What is the difference between home and school, from a child's point of view? What does it mean to become a pupil? These difficult but important questions can be thought about in many ways. Physically, emotionally, socially and cognitively, clearly home and school are two entirely different worlds. How can schools make sense to children?

Let us look at these ways separately. In physical terms the school building is likely to feel entirely different, being enormous and puzzling by comparison with home, and with the areas inhabited by children designed for very different purposes. (Those areas that children are used to at home – the kitchen and the living room [at school, the staff room] – are in any case out of bounds to pupils, and as for bedrooms, of course they do not feature.) On the other hand, on the whole the furniture and equipment is the right size for children, rather than being designed for adults. So in visual terms, a sense of unfamiliarity is inevitable until the child becomes used to this very different environment.

In emotional terms, for the 'new' child there may be a seismic shock in terms of identity. This transition carries all the implications of the change from being 'a big fish in a little pond', to 'a little fish in a very big pond'. This process comes at a time when children are struggling to understand how they are perceived by the people around them, and it is hardly surprising when they find it profoundly un-settling. It is thought-provoking to consider what are the messages that a child receives about his or her place in this new order of things, right from the start. The answers to the 'identity' questions in the child's mind: 'Am I important? Likeable? Reliable? Good?' depend to a large extent in the school context on how he or she is received at the beginning of the first term, and on those early interactions between children and teachers. Practical arrangements also carry hidden messages for children about their worth; first or last in the playground queue, accessibility of the toilets, and so on. Much is also gleaned by children from teachers' body language, a much more reliable 'barometer' for young children than what is said. And of course sharing your 'mother substitute'/teacher with 20 to 30 other children can be enormously challenging, even for those children who have previously been able to make a range of attachments with key workers in day-care.

The adult–child ratio necessarily results in very different kinds of interactions at school between children and their 'important adults'. But it is also important to remember those children who are vulnerable at home, and for whom schools and settings can be the 'safe haven' that they need. Schools cannot always know which children these are, and so this consideration makes the welcome that all children receive at school even more important.

Socially, the challenges are enormous. At home, relationships are a 'given', built on the foundations of very many shared experiences for as long as a child can remember. Even where these are problematic, a child usually learns coping strategies. When starting school, there are so many new relationships to make. No wonder opportunities to make friends before starting school is valued by children and families, and no wonder the advantage of starting school with friends is one that usually matters very much to children. All these considerations of unfamiliarity and challenge highlight the many advantages of strategies that enable children to begin some of this work before the first 'proper' day at school. To let children become familiar with the building, to have spent time in the social milieu of the classroom, and had conversations with the teacher, makes a great deal of difference to how that first 'proper' day goes.

Cognitively the world of school is likely to be enormously different too. At home, children are likely to be used to asking the questions of adults, who mostly provide some sort of answer. But schools tend to be the other way around, with teachers asking the questions, and children expected to provide the answers. This is made all the more confusing by the fact that so often teachers clearly already know the answers to the questions they are asking (for instance 'what colour is your coat?'). As Nel Noddings says (2003, p. 31), 'I don't think schools kill curiosity and creativity in everything they do, but it is a near thing'.

But what of the other side of the coin? This glimpse of the challenges of starting school would not be complete without including the way that very many schools manage to make the transition into school a positive and exciting experience, resulting in a huge increase in children's confidence and competence. There are many ways that schools do this, often including a skilful partnership with parents who, rather than merely being helpless onlookers, become key people in the process. There is more about how this can work, in Chapter 12.

– THE TREASURE HUNT –

❝ Lily's really made friends with Lisa. I think she wanted to make sure that Lisa is interested in her too, so she's been showing her lots of things that she likes doing. Yesterday Lily wanted Lisa to play with her, and it was all right because I played with Joe so they could get on with it – but I kept an eye on what they did, when I could. First they read the Treasure Hunt book together and then Lily wanted Lisa to help her make up a Treasure Hunt in the garden. Lisa said Dan was coming to tea so they could do it for when he comes, and that's what they did.

Lisa said Lily was really fed up at first because they had to read and write things and it was difficult for Lily and at first she couldn't see the point. But then when she saw that the messages were how you did the Treasure Hunt, she stopped fussing and explained it all to Dan when he came. In the end they had a great time, especially as Lisa made sure they both found some treasure. Mum told Lisa what they could use, and Dan's treasure was a little car that was in the bottom of the toy-box. Lily said he could take it home if he liked. Her treasure was a book about babies that someone gave her ages ago when Joe was born and she had forgotten all about it. Now she thinks it's great because after a couple of times she could remember every page.

As soon as Lily's dad got home Lily had to tell him all about it. When he said 'What was the Treasure then?' she showed him her book about babies, and he and Mum laughed at the idea of her thinking babies were treasures when she gets so cross with Joe. But she said now she's grown-up and knows about why you do reading and writing and things, she doesn't mind about Joe. She says when she goes to Big School she can explain grown-up things to him, like Lisa did to her today. I wonder what he'll think of that?❞

Talking, listening, playing and singing together, and sharing books every day . . . from birth all children need opportunities to do these things, with people they love and admire who recognise, value and encourage their efforts and achievements

Children's companions

As Judy Dunn (2004, p. 34) points out, when they start school 'all children, after all, now have choice in who they play with or talk to. The new question is, will they choose me?'. This is a very different situation from the one at home, where for the most part children's companions are not of their choosing. However, children's experience of companionship at home is likely to make a considerable impact on their expectations, responses and relationships with school companions, whether children or adults.

Sometimes it can seem as though, as children start school, their previous companions such as parents, siblings and extended family might become less important. But this is exactly the time when children need the knowledge that those familiar companions are still there for them, even while they are making new friends. This is part of children's need for continuity and consistence mentioned earlier. So if anything, extra time will be needed with important people, to reassure that all is still well in the world, and that new experiences and challenges will not undermine the earliest long-standing companionships which generate the foundations of identity and confidence.

In Chapter 1, the way in which a baby's self-concept develops is described as a mirroring process between the mother and the baby; and this process continues with children's 'important' adults and peers at school, in relation to their self-esteem. Below are some statements about children's developing self-esteem that repay some reflection as we think about them in the context of the reception class. This is the 'mirroring' process in action, as important in settings for young children as in the home.

High self-esteem comes from:
- *Realising that others like your ideas and will follow your lead*
- *Always being warmly accepted as a person in your own world*
- *People's willingness to listen and take you seriously*
- *Feeling that other people enjoy being with you; this feeling comes from frequently being enjoyed*
- *Being acknowledged and appreciated for exactly who you are*
- *Doing things that you find interesting and important*
- *Knowing you can trust people to be concerned about your feelings and needs*
- *Experiencing time and time again, year in and year out, that the important people in your life take time just for you – to listen, to explain things, to relax with you, to share confidences, to find moments every day in which friendship can flourish*

These statements offer an opportunity to review the likely impact on children's self-esteem as they start school. Reversing them offers a very gloomy picture for self-esteem prospects, e.g. 'low self-esteem comes from realising that others do not like your ideas or do not follow your lead' etc. And while early childhood care and education settings and primary schools are the kinds of places where these statements are valued, it is worth thinking about exactly how children might (or perhaps might not) be receiving these messages, especially in the first days and weeks at school.

Learning together

Talking and listening, playing and singing together, and sharing books every day – these are things that are associated with early childhood both at home and in care and education settings. Or at least, talking and listening, playing and singing, and sharing books are. It is the rest of the statement for this section that is challenging, because while in families talking and listening, playing and singing, and sharing books do tend to happen together with people children love and admire, at school this is more difficult to achieve, and is not necessarily part of the picture.

At home there is so much that children learn simply by being with their 'important' people. They learn from sharing routines, from being part of everyday activities, from going out and exploring the world together. And the youngest children in our schools still need this element of close relationship for their learning. In relation to transitions, the especially challenging word in this statement is the word 'recognise'. This implies that the child is well known, so that valuing and encouraging can naturally follow. But at the outset children cannot be well known, a precious situation that develops over time.

This leaves a precarious period when, with the best will in the world, a teacher's praise and encouragement may well be inappropriately too much or too little. It has long been recognised that the better a teacher knows the children, the better the learning and teaching will be. Now we know that this same recognition applies to children's emotional development, and that the better a teacher knows a child, the better the child's emotional stability will be. Praise and encouragement that is based on knowledge of a child's recent efforts and achievements will help that child to feel more secure. But how can this knowledge be gained as quickly as possible by schools wanting to ease transition? Chapter 12 contains some strategies.

The magic of books

A wonderful way to spend time together is in book-sharing. Children love the affectionate physical proximity and the undivided attention that is involved in cuddling up with a book, and children who have had this experience all of their lives at home are very fortunate. But some children experience this for the first time at school, where it can also be enormously reassuring (although harder to achieve the one-to-one opportunities needed). At home or at school, this may be a perfect introduction to the sort of conversations discussed earlier, when children are needing to talk about things that have happened, to share feelings and to ask questions.

Sharing books regularly with very young children has so many benefits; and with the explosion in quality publishing for very young children, it's not only the child who has a good time. Here are some benefits for language acquisition listed by the National Book Trust (www.talktoyourbaby.org.uk):

- It's fun
- It helps develop social and literacy skills, and encourages two-way communication
- Babies love the sound of their parents' voices and reading aloud to them can be a calming, soothing experience which helps build the bond between carer and child
- Books introduce children to the exciting world of stories and help them to learn to express their own thoughts and emotions
- Stories provide parents and carers with a structure to help them talk aloud to children and listen to their responses
- Reading together gives babies and young children a chance to respond
- Characters, words and sounds discovered through books can be talked about at other times
- Songs and rhymes are especially good for children as the rhymes and repetitive language make it easier for babies to learn language sklls
- Reading aloud combines the benefits of talking, listening and storytelling within a single activity
- Reading to babies and young children, and giving them time to respond, will help make the most of brain development at this time

As well as all these benefits, cuddling up and sharing books right from the start helps children to grow up with a love of books that is enormously important and helpful as they enter school. It is the best way to help them enjoy books and become readers, a focus of so much of the earliest years at school. There are so many kinds of books too, many of them suitable for even the youngest 'reader'; and beautifully produced with wonderful illustrations that add enormously to the conversational possibilities. These include story books, song and nursery rhyme books, board and vinyl books, playbooks with flaps, moving parts and noises, rhyming books and books with repeated words, picture books with drawings or photos of familiar things, and books about everyday life and special occasions. In these books a whole new world opens up, of stories, songs and rhymes, humour and nonsense, drawings and photographs, colours and shapes, fact and fantasy, and information.

Another firm favourite with young children is home-made books that they have helped to make, especially books about themselves. Making a book about starting school can be a good way into the conversations that might be helpful. These home-made books can be tiny or giant, with photographs and drawings, and messages from the child to the reader. This is a great way to give a child a sense of authorship, so that all the effort of learning to read and write makes sense! And children learn a lot about reading and writing from the people around them, in particular they quickly pick up whether this activity generates pleasure or perhaps is felt to be tedious. Children who know that their important adults read and write for pleasure are more likely to want very much to be able to do it themselves.

And children love to be able to choose their own books, perhaps from a shelf at home or at school, or maybe from the library. Here is a list of things, collected by the PEEP project, that children love about starting reading on their own:

- Having a shelf of books within easy reach
- Having a place to curl up and look at books
- Choosing books themselves
- Holding the book and turning the pages
- Looking at books by themselves and with friends
- Joining in with a story
- Remembering the words on some books
- Telling and acting out a story – preferably with an audience!
(Roberts, 2000a)

These are just some of the reasons for making the very most of opportunities to share books with young children, together with a glimpse of their perspective on it. Book sharing in all its diversity needs to be more widely promoted, not only at home but in all early childhood care and education settings. There is so much to be gained, both for children and for adults. It is puzzling that this very rich vein of early childhood education and care is still for the most part (and of course with notable exceptions) so unexplored.

– VISITING DAN –

❛ Dan's off to Big School after the summer – and just before the end of term he had to go and look at his classroom and see his teacher. Lily and Mum went with him to drop him off. Mum said that now Lily has seen where Dan will be, she can look forward to going there too, after Christmas. But Lily said she didn't want to go, and Mum said why not? Lily didn't answer; but I think she is jealous of Dan, and feeling angry because he's going without her. Anyway Mum said not to worry, they'd be going to collect Dan lots of times next term so she'd soon get used to it. And Mum said she was going to help Dan's teacher sometimes and Lily could come too if she liked. Then Lily really cheered up, because she saw the home corner in Dan's classroom and she really wants to play in it.

Next time Lily played with Dan she asked him about Big School and what it was like. He told her it was different from Nursery and there are lots of bigger children and you have to sit down and do things, and then you go out to the playground, and you have *dinner in the big hall and it's very noisy. I asked him about the teacher, and he said the teacher is very nice and she asked him a lot of questions. And he likes learning how to read like the big children, but he doesn't want to get lost going from the playground to the classroom. And he wants to take a lunch-box because if you have school dinners you have to remember which table you are sitting on and he's worried about forgetting. So Lily said she wants a lunch-box too – I wonder what Mum will say?*

Dan told us about two boys who are friends and talk to each other in another language when they are playing in the home corner (I heard the teacher tell Mum it's Punjabi) but they listen to the teacher when she talks in English and one of them told Dan in English where to find something he wanted. They have a sort of sign language as well, and lots of the other children can do that too. Dan says the teacher taught them. Dan says it's really clever to talk in another language, and he wants to talk in two languages too.

Lisa told me she thinks Mum is really good to help Dan's teacher, because at College they tell you that parents and teachers need to get to know each other. Then they can talk about their children's learning and progress. And children need to get used to school too, before they start, so what Mum's doing is a good way. She said seeing parents and teachers talking together helps children to feel safe at school, and then they want to get on with learning. ❯

Wanting to learn makes all the difference to success

Learning dispositions

Not only has there recently been an increasing acknowledgement of the extraordinary competence of very young children, but also we have seen an important expansion in the view of the curriculum itself, in which children's personal, social and emotional areas of development are all acknowledged. However, children's learning *dispositions* are not yet widely recognised as an important goal of education. But here is how Lilian Katz (1993, p. 1) saw it:

One of the major questions to be addressed when developing a curriculum is, What should be learned? One way to answer this question . . . is to adopt at least four types of learning goals, those related to knowledge, skills, dispositions and feelings. The acquisition of both knowledge and skills is taken for granted as an educational goal, and most educators would also readily agree that many feelings (e.g. self-esteem) are also influenced by school experiences and are thus worthy of inclusion among learning goals. However, dispositions are seldom included, although they are often implied by the inclusion of attitudes (e.g. attitudes towards learning) as goals . . . it is possible to have skills and lack a taste for or habit of using them. Similarly, knowledge can be acquired without having the disposition to use it.

What difference would it make to the way early years care and education settings and schools operate if the first and most important question to be asked in formal school assessments was 'Does this child want to learn here?' What would be the impact on education in our fast-changing world if positive learning dispositions were seen as *the* goal of twenty-first-century education?

The question of children's learning dispositions is an important one that has been explored in a variety of ways, especially by Sylva (1994) and Katz (1995). Positive learning dispositions have been seen as relating to such factors as exploring, experimenting, persisting, learning from mistakes, questioning, watching and listening. In her book *Assessment in Early Childhood Settings* Margaret Carr (2001, p. 23), in the context of early childhood in New Zealand, analysed the domains of learning dispositions as:

- taking an interest
- being involved
- persisting with difficulty or uncertainty
- communicating with others
- taking responsibility

Taking this analysis a step further, she proposes the categories of 'being ready', 'being willing', and 'being able', fitting the domains listed above into these stages of development. Anyone engaged in supporting young children's learning will recognise the relevance of, say, being ready to take an interest, being willing to take an interest, and being able to do so; and of being ready, willing and able to communicate, and so on. This altogether new way of looking at outcomes of early childhood education and care is a thought-provoking alternative to the usual categories of language, mathematics, etc. Here, for example, is how being ready, willing and able to persist with difficulty or uncertainty (an area closely related to self-esteem) is described:

- Readiness to persist, in which children are developing: enthusiasm for persisting with difficulty or uncertainty; assumptions about risk and the role of making a mistake in learning; a view of self as someone who persists with difficulty and uncertainty.
- Willingness to persist, in which children are developing: sensitivity to places and occasions in which it is worth while to tackle difficulty or uncertainty and to resist the routine.
- Ability to persist, in which children are developing: problem-solving and problem-finding knowledge and skills; experience of making mistakes as part of solving a problem.

This thinking highlights the complexity of learning dispositions, indicating some of the important elements contained within the simple question of whether or not a child wants to learn, and why. Christine Pascal (2003) writes illuminatingly about 'attitudes and dispositions to learn', identifying these as one of three domains of effective early learning (the others are emotional well-being, and social competence/self-concept). Describing attitudes and dispositions to learn as 'behavioural characteristics and attitudes', Pascal proposes four key elements: independence, creativity, self-motivation and resilience. While these models of learning dispositions vary in certain respects, they have a common focus not on content or outcomes, but rather on the vital *processes* of learning.

Babies and young children have all the readiness, willingness and ability to learn in the world, and it is our job as adults to support them in further developing their abilities. But as 'schooling' – or is it conformity? – gets under way, a process of erosion seems to take place which eats away at these dispositions. During the course of these first years at school, what becomes of that powerful curiosity, exploration, observation, questioning, persistence, concentration? This erosion may have as much to do with processes of social and emotional development as it does with cognitive functioning, and yet we need to ask ourselves what it is about our education systems that allows this to happen.

There has been an assumption that it should be the task of practitioners to plan for 'supporting, fostering, promoting and developing children's . . . positive attitudes and learning dispositions' (QCA/DfES, 2000, p. 8). This has been to imply that learning dispositions need to be 'taught'. But to use an architectural analogy, children's learning dispositions are not 'new build', they are 'conservation'. Maybe we should be thinking about this rather differently. Rather than 'new build' (with its accompanying requirement for all the complexities of education's equivalent to planning permission) perhaps we should be planning for the architectural equivalent of 'conservation': ensuring instead that by observing, valuing, protecting and supporting children's positive attitudes and dispositions to learn, we enable them to thrive.

Throughout this book the reader has been reminded of Lily's and Joe's learning dispositions. In common with the vast majority of children in their early years, Lily and Joe and their friends are voracious learners. Anyone who has lived with a baby or a toddler will recognise the boundless curiosity, the extraordinary powers of observation, the relentless questioning, the often maddening persistence, the sometimes obsessive concentration. These are the characteristics of successful learners, and it is hardly surprising that the youngest children display them in such strength when we consider what an enormous amount it is that children of this age are learning. On the 'half empty' or 'half full' model, when it comes to learning dispositions these children are overflowing. The important question here is not about how to 'teach' children to learn, but – much more crucially – about how *not* to stop them.

12

Supporting children's journeys

– LILY STARTS SCHOOL –

❛Today was Lily's first day at school. There was a real big fuss yesterday because Lily said that Dan said you have to have a special lunch-box, and she only had her old one that she and Dan used to play picnics with. She got in such a state that Mum went out and got another one, and Dad said it was ridiculous and he thought the teacher wouldn't mind what she brought her lunch in – but Lily minded. After that she was all ready, and she really wanted to go because Dan said they were going to do something special on the first day for all the new children.

When Lily came home she told us all about it. She said lots of people at school said hello and smiled at her. Lisa asked was that the children, or the teachers, or both? Lily said it was both, and the dinner ladies and everybody, and they all seemed to know it was her first day. Lisa said what a good idea, to tell absolutely everybody in the school to look after the new children and be nice to them. Then Lily said that all the new children had a special person in the class to look after them for the first few days, and show them where to find things and what to do; and we had to guess who her special person was. I said how could we do that when we didn't know the people in the class? But Lily just stood there smiling at us, with her eyes all shiny, and then Lisa said 'I know, it's Dan!'

At tea-time Lily told us about a special game they played, that the other children had got ready the day before. All the new children played it with their special person, so Lily did it with Dan. She said it was a kind of treasure hunt and they had to go all over the school to find things. She said now she knows how to find all the places so she can't get lost, can she? And she told us about when she was eating her packed lunch, and she was sitting next to a big boy in Year 6 and he gave her some of his chocolate cake! Mum said 'Did he talk to you?' and Lily said yes, he asked her if she likes Big School. Her dad grinned and said 'What did you tell him Lily?' And she grinned back and said 'Yes!'

Mum and their dad were talking about Lily tonight after she was in bed. They were nearly having an argument because Mum was worried that Lily's bossy and when she starts organising people and asking lots of questions she might get into trouble and not be happy. Their dad said all mums worry too much about their children going to school, and he thought if anyone was going to do all right it was Lily. Mum asked what was so great about Lily then? And their dad suddenly got really serious and fierce and *said 'I'll tell you what's great about her. She wants to know things, and she doesn't give up, and she really likes other people. She's a cracker is our Lily, and don't you forget it!' Then Mum cried and he hugged her, and me and Lisa went out.* **❯**

Children in transition need to know what to expect, with *time* and *support* to reflect on their experiences and to look forward to new ones; and *confidence* that adults will understand and respect their needs

Making the most of childhood

Chapter 11's second section, entitled '"Properly" being four', argued that the best preparation for being five is to have properly been four, and before that three, and so on. This chapter focuses on an adult perspective of children's transitions, and has the same starting-point. There has been a dismaying (though of course not universal) tendency in families, settings, schools and government departments to view early childhood as a preparation for later childhood and ultimately for adulthood. But while there is increasing evidence that the situations and experiences of early childhood make a long-term impact on later outcomes, childhood is not a rehearsal; and children are four (and three, etc.) only once. So, in a general sense, the best way to prepare children for things to come is to make the very most of each day – after all, it will never come again. This 'making the most of childhood' has been the main rationale for each section of the book; this is what lies behind self-esteem and early learning.

In this final chapter the main ideas in previous sections of the book are reviewed. Starting with Lily's first day at school and her parents' whole-hearted involvement and interest in her experiences, it tracks back to the foundations beneath Lily's cheerful account and her parents' tensions as she starts school; uncovering the layers of their situations and experiences together, right from the very beginning. But first there are two sections: on the important shift to more integrated services in early childhood education and care; and on babies and young children's need for strong attachments, from birth right through to school. Also interspersed through this last chapter are a series of more practical sections about how adults can ease children's transitions into school.

A holistic view of services

In Chapter 11 a holistic view of children was promoted. Such a view carries implications for the services that support the youngest children and their families. It is very helpful for families – especially bi-lingual families and also those with additional needs who will need support from a range of sources – if those services are able to co-ordinate and work together. Without such co-ordination, families already under pressure can feel harassed and discouraged by the number of service-providers with whom they are in contact. In such circumstances it is difficult for parents to feel any sense of ownership or control over the identification of problems, or their solutions.

One way of dealing with this in the UK has been the development of integrated services to support children and families. Such services offer a much more satisfactory way of supporting families with the youngest children, aiming to make a difference to children's physical development, their social and emotional development, how they learn, and school readiness. They also aim to strengthen families and communities in a variety of ways including by working together with shared aims, objectives and targets. This integrated approach to supporting families is underpinning the development of many new collaborative strategies in the UK, with the intention of changing radically the provision that is offered to families.

Children's Centres such as Pen Green and Coram Family have been blazing this trail for many years, working inspirationally to meet the needs of families and young children in a holistic way (Whalley, 1997). In this new way of working, health visitors, schools, centres and voluntary bodies come together, providing a more 'seamless' service for children and families. Much is being learned from this work, which provides opportunities to identify those elements that are most effective in supporting families with the youngest children.

Children in transition need strong attachments

Young children need to be cared for by people who they know will provide them with safety, warmth and comfort, and to these people they become 'attached'. Much has been written about attachment theory and its importance in the relationship between the baby and the mother (and sometimes other primary carers, often the father). Attachment is sometimes described as being like a piece of invisible elastic, attached at one end to the child and at the other to the child's primary carer. A 'well-attached' child is able to play happily in the proximity of the carer, sometimes moving away and sometimes returning for visual or close physical contact. It is as if the invisible elastic between them can stretch to a certain extent, but not too far or it will break. The stronger the attachment, the more stretchy the elastic! When a primary carer hands over the care of the child to a 'substitute' primary carer (as in day-care) children need to transfer the 'elastic' process to the new person; and this of course can only be done when a new relationship is made, that is based on trust.

A crucial element of young children's experience of transition is this one of transferring attachment. Success depends on the opportunities that both the child and the new adult have at the outset, to make this vital new relationship based on trust. For most babies and young children who are well attached to their initial primary carer, in the earliest years there follow a series of other attachments. These are usually made with a grandparent or other family member, a child-minder, or a 'key person' in a day-care setting. In these additional, crucially important relationships, the child is learning to transfer the skills and expectations learned in the initial attachment relationship, to other people. These early attachment relationships lay the foundations for all the child's later close relationships – and the critical time for their successful development is during the transition period from one situation to another. At this time, babies and young children are most likely to be able to make a trusting relationship with adults who are sensitive, warm, responsive and consistent; and regularly and reliably available. They need to learn that if they feel anxious, this person will respond in a way that helps them to feel secure.

Sometimes people working in day-care – and indeed parents – fear that a new attachment may come to replace an existing one. Workers may worry that making a close and trusting relationship with a child might detract from the child's relationships at home; and parents sometimes fear that if their child grows close to another carer, the love they themselves will receive from the child may be less. These fears are based on a belief that more than one close attachment at a time is not possible, and that a child only has a limited amount of love to 'share out'.

But this is not how it works. Babies who experience strong attachments are better able to make new ones *at the same time as* strengthening existing ones. It can even be argued that when an attachment with a mother is vulnerable (as can happen for so many reasons) a strong attachment formed in day-care can help the mother, through the way that the baby or young child comes to understand what a strong attachment means and how it works. The baby's positive experience in day-care can help to strengthen a vulnerable relationship at home.

Many of the early situations and experiences described in Part I of this book are relevant to attachment. Chapter 1 (the child's perspective) includes babies' earliest learning, their need for 'containment', and the importance of their carers' unconditional acceptance. The chapter goes on to look at the processes of the early development of self-concept as the foundation of a child's self-esteem; and to investigate the links between self-concept and behaviour. Chapter 2 is about adults' perspective of these issues. What helps adults to deal with babies' needs for containment and acceptance? Why is it that a primary carer's knowledge and understanding of a baby or young child is so vitally important? What are the things that adults can do to support babies' developing self-concept, with its implications for their self-esteem and wider development? All these aspects are vital to the health and well-being of a baby in the first year of life; and they are also highly relevant to the way in which a child subsequently manages the normal transitions of early childhood.

Long-term fundamental feelings

In a review of policies in the UK to support the well-being of young children (Scott and Ward, 2005), Gillian Pugh summarises key risk and protective factors for children, emphasising the importance of secure attachment. Protective factors in parents included the following:

- Warm, affectionate relationships
- Predictability and consistency
- Open and effective communication
- Time spent together
- Clear limit setting
- Empathy
- Support for education

These factors are repeatedly reflected in all the sections above, as is the following conclusion:

> *Positive, nurturing relationships between children and parents, and parents' ability to see the world through the eyes of their children or put themselves in their shoes, provide the crucial foundation for a secure and well adjusted future.* (Pugh, in Scott and Ward, 2005)

This 'seeing the world through the eyes of their children' is the basis of all the 'odd number' chapters in this book (1, 3, 5, 7 and 9) and is particularly important in Chapter 3 of Part 2 ('Fundamental feelings'), which outlines much of the basis for later mental health. The examination of 'normal' bad feelings focuses on the many experiences in the very earliest years that are so hard for babies and young children to manage, arguing that in order for children and young people to learn to manage the normal ups and downs of life, they need their responses to these early experiences to be seen by their 'important' adults as normal and acceptable. Babies and young children need to be allowed to cry, protest and be unhappy when they need to. This is hard for adults, whose tendency is to want children to be happy. Chapters 3 and 4 emphasise how important it is for adults to give babies and young children time to experience these feelings with acceptance, understanding and sympathy; and suggest ways of thinking about them which can be helpful.

Knowing what to expect is very important for children too. This is partly about the time factor again, with adults willing and able to explain to children what is going to happen. Knowing what to expect is also about continuity and consistency, both important aspects of learning about other people.

Saying 'yes' and saying 'no'

The section earlier in this chapter on the importance of attachment is an important precursor to learning about other people. A baby's attachment to the primary carer(s) lays the foundations for later relationships with others in the family, and the world outside. In Part 3 ('About other people') Chapter 5 we have seen Lily's preoccupation with her dolls, her developing relationship with her younger brother, and the eventful shopping expedition with their dad. In all these anecdotes Lily is beginning to learn about other people and her world, and about expectations and rules. At the beginning of Chapter 6 the focus is on Joe, who is having a tea-time protest. Then there are arguments between Mum and Lily about biscuits and about television, and a difficult time for Lily's friend Dan who comes to play with Lily and drops a precious pot of Mum's. Here the commentary is about how adults deal with situations involving setting limits, being consistent, dealing with tantrums, and managing those important but often difficult times when children so urgently need to feel independent.

In all these situations a helpful guiding principle might be:

> *SAY 'YES' AS OFTEN AS YOU CAN,*
> *AND WHEN YOU SAY 'NO', MEAN IT*

It is not unusual to hear or read the second part of this maxim, which is a well-established and entirely sensible (though sometimes easier-said-than-done) approach to behaviour management. Penelope Leach (2003, p. 535) writes:

> *Children need adults who have the courage of their convictions and the courage to set limits and draw boundaries for them, within which they know they can stay safe – and good . . . to keep them safe while they learn to keep themselves safe; to control them while they develop self-control, and to make sure they don't lose their own space or trespass on other people's while they learn the lessons of socialised living like 'do as you would be done by'.*

And she goes on to say:

> *Limits are only limits if children cannot break them. And they only give children safe freedom of action if they know they cannot . . . If you set a limit, make sure the child cannot overstep it.* (p. 535)

But what about the first half of the principle? 'Say "yes" as often as you can' sounds so obvious that surely we all do it? In fact this is not the case; and it is just when things are getting difficult that it is hardest to remember about saying 'yes' – because that is just when the inclination is more and more to say 'no'. However, in terms of positive prevention, saying 'yes' as often as you can is a great strategy. It gives children a sense of acceptance, approval and freedom; and it positively reinforces adults' sense of well-being. And if saying 'yes' seems to have gone out of the window, it's not hard to get it back because you can always suggest something a child would like, to which you are willing to agree! It is almost as though the number of times you can say 'yes' directly reduces the number of times you have to say 'no'.

This 'yes' strategy is a very useful one in times of transition. Because 'yes' is usually associated with approval, it helps to reduce children's tension and increases their confidence. And developing a pattern of saying 'yes' goes some way to help reduce adult tensions too.

– MUM DOES IT RIGHT! –

❛ *Every week Mum takes Joe to a sort of singing group where they do lots of stories and playing, and sometimes I go too. It's really for Joe, but Lily likes going too – she loves the baby songs and stories, and I think it makes her feel grown-up and clever because she helps.*

The other day Lily found a really good folder that came from the group, with ideas and stories and games . . . and when Mum looked at it with Lisa she laughed because there was a game in there about having a cardboard box with a hole in it and the baby puts things in and then takes the lid off and takes them out and does it all over again. She said it was Joe's favourite game for months and the cheapest toy he'd ever had. Then she looked at some more things in the folder and she was smiling. She said perhaps she'd done it right with Lily after all, and it was nice to see all the things in a book. She said all that stuff they did together really helped when it came to getting Lily ready for school. Then Lily got cross and said SHE did things right, not Mum. She's been at school a couple of weeks and she's cross quite a lot these days. Mum says maybe it's because she's feeling tired after school and it's a big effort even though she seems to be doing fine. She says we must all be extra kind to Lily for a bit.

That evening when we were all sitting round and Lily was in bed, Mum said she felt like wanting someone to be extra kind to her, as well. She said when Lily was at Nursery, most days nearly all the parents used to have a little chat with the teacher or someone, but now Lily's at big school it's different, and Mum really misses not knowing how she's getting on and the conversations she and Lily used to have. Lily doesn't talk about what's happened at school, like she did then – maybe she's too tired at the end of the day, or maybe she thinks Mum won't understand. Mum says she wishes she could have a very quick chat with Lily's teacher now and then at the end of the day, but as it is she'll have to wait until the parents' meeting – unless there's a problem 'and I wouldn't want that to happen' she said, holding on to the wooden table-leg! She said that before Lily started, the school and Lily's Nursery talked to her as well as each other a lot, and they were really helpful about what parents needed to know. Now they still send notices and things in Lily's book bag – but Mum said now Lily's actually started, she feels invisible.

Lily's dad said Mum's got to learn to let go, but Mum said chats now and then with the teacher are just what would help her to let go. Lisa said schools want parents to be involved with their children's learning, and isn't it hard to help your child if you don't really know how the teacher thinks they're getting on? And I said I miss the way Lily used to talk to us about her day too, so I agree with Mum. Then their dad said if we all go on listening to Lily and doing lots of things with her it'll all be fine, and how about Lily and all of us having a day out while Lisa's here? So we all started saying where we wanted to go and getting excited, until their dad said he thought Mum should choose . . . but hadn't we better consult the child herself? Then we all laughed and Mum said she felt better.

> **Talking, listening, playing and singing together, and sharing books every day . . . from birth all children need opportunities to do these things, with people they love and admire who recognise, value and encourage their efforts and achievements**

How can parents help?

Years of consulting parents about their own and their children's needs indicates that the following factors seem to matter most:

- Happiness
- Health
- Confidence
- Independence

More recent consultations with children reveal the following worries about starting school:

- What will the playground be like?
- Will they like me?
- What if I feel ill?
- Will I be all right at lunch-time?
- What happens if I get into trouble?
- When will I be allowed to play (like I did at my nursery)?
- Where are the toilets?
- Will I be too slow changing for PE?
- Will I get lost?

Children need reassurance, and information about what to expect. Knowing the answers to at least some of these sorts of questions will go a long way to making sure that children have the four factors that parents mostly want for them.

This section examines what adults can do to help transitions go smoothly, particularly in relation to starting school. In the family narrative above, Lily's mum is having a hard time too; and so the perspective below widens to include what can be done to help parents and families as well as children themselves.

The parent or main carer is the central person for the child in the external world as well as the internal one of the home. In the child's rapidly expanding world the parent or main carer is the *continuity* person, a child specialist in relation to *this* child. He or she will also know the people who provide services – the health visitor, the child-minder, the day-care supervisor, the pre-school leader, the family centre staff, the teacher. Parents' co-ordinating role can be a crucial one, and many services work hard to acknowledge this, to make the most of it and to support parents and carers in it. In 2000, the UK government had this to say about parents:

> *Parents are children's first and most enduring educators. When parents and practitioners work together in early years settings, the results have a positive impact on the child's development and learning. Therefore, each setting should seek to develop an effective partnership with parents. A successful partnership needs a two-way flow of information, knowledge and expertise.* (QCA/DfES, 2000, p. 9)

In the same year a Sure Start booklet confirmed:

> *A strong relationship with parents encourages continuity for the child, good communication, participation and ownership. In order to be involved, parents must have information.* (Sure Start, 2000a, p. 24)

This theme had been taken up by the PEEP project in the 'Learning Together' series (Roberts, 2000a), working with parents about supporting their children's self-esteem and learning dispositions, as well as children's very early literacy and numeracy development. This is how the PEEP model (originally developed with parents in Sheffield, see Hannon, 1995) appears in the introductory section of the 'Learning Together' folders:

> *'Learning Together' covers the time from birth to school . . . It is based on four main ideas:*
>
> - *Opportunities for learning and all-round development in everyday life*
> - *Recognising and valuing children's efforts and achievements day by day*
> - *Interactive everyday activities and experiences to do together*
> - *Modelling or setting an example by adults can make all the difference*

The introduction continues with a letter to parents:

> *Dear Parents,*
> *Being a parent is one of the most vital, and one of the most undervalued jobs in the world. We believe that you are your child's first and most important educators. Now we know how parents can help their children make a flying start at school. Here are some of the things that make a real difference, right from the start: sharing a book*

every day, lots of songs and rhymes, listening games, playing with shapes and belong-ing to the library. Libraries love baby members!

When children start school, the support parents have given them – and continue to give them over the years – enormously influences their achievements. These folders explain how you can give that support to your child as a natural part of everyday life. They offer information and ideas, as well as showing you what a good job you are doing already. The most important part of using 'Learning Together' is the fun of talking, listening, playing, singing and sharing books together, and the confidence that it brings to parents and children.

The focus here is on what parents and carers already do every day, offering them information and ideas about supporting their children's development. This approach is an important addition to the 'getting ready for school' strategies that can be helpful as the time for 'Big School' approaches.

Knowing what will help each particular child to make a flying start at school and grow into a competent, confident adult is clearly a complicated business, and depends to a large extent on the particular needs of the individual child and the expertise of parents and carers. The EPPE project (Sammons *et al.*, 1999) has shown that when children have had certain experiences in the earliest years at home, they will be in a better position to learn at school in the UK education system. Until recently it was thought that the strongest predictors of children's later achieve-ments were the level of their parents' education, especially the mother's; and par-ents' occupational status. These are still known to be significant, but five other experiences were found to be more important, even after parents' education and occupational status had been taken into account. The experiences are: regular book-sharing; regular library visits; playing with letters or numbers; learning the alpha-bet; knowing various songs and rhymes.

This list will not come as a surprise to people who are living and working with young children. 'Well we knew that already!' can be the response to findings that seem to confirm our common sense. It is important, however, that such findings can be put forward as the result of solid evidence rather than as a kind of folklore. Children's care and education must be based on a careful synthesis of the body of evidence we have, if we are to avoid placing them at the mercy of the winds of edu-cation 'fashion' and political change.

Below is a list of broader characteristics and abilities (Roberts, 2000a), that parents and schools acknowledge as being generally helpful when it comes to starting school:

- Communicating well
- Listening carefully
- Talking to other people outside the family
- Respecting and getting on with other people, with good manners
- Asking questions

- Accepting a routine
- Knowing what to expect
- Saying what they need
- Coping with surrounding noise and activity

Most of these things build up over time, the results of many many small family experiences where they can be practised. These things can be developed as part of the normal day-to-day life for children in any family, in any race or culture. 'Knowing what to expect' is different in that it requires specific information, and this is why it is helpful if parents can find out all they can about what it will be like for their children as they start school. Parents can help children come to terms with what to expect in very practical ways, as long as the school helps with this strategy. There is more about this in the section below about how schools can help.

Like 'knowing what to expect', physical independence is another enormously important factor influencing how smoothly a child starts school. Being able to manage your own clothes and find your way around the building is an important element of life at school, to say nothing of managing the toilet. Writing for parents, Leach (2003, p. 549) advises:

> Go for shoes with Velcro instead of knot-prone laces; make sure that dressing and undressing herself is a daily routine she takes for-granted, and check that the new items she's proud of – such as her lunch box and school bag – are easily opened. It's worth finding her opportunities to practise any school-techniques which will be new to her, too, such as drinking from a drinking fountain or finding the coat-hook with her name on it. A child who copes confidently with these everyday matters saves the teacher time and trouble but she saves herself something even more important: anxiety.

As Leach says:

> A sense of being able to cope with all that's expected is a vital part of self-confidence for all of us, at any time . . . you can equip your child with school clothes and a school bag the day before she starts, but confidence and competence take longer.

Finally, where does it all end? Certainly not on the first day of primary school. Parents can make a big difference to their children by carrying on helping every day – by doing things together, noticing and praising progress, talking and listening together, and being a good example. But at the same time, children need to know that it is safe for them to acquire a new 'school life' and that by doing so they will not be risking their special 'attachments' at home. Parents can help with this too . . . by managing to 'let go' to some extent, while at the same time making sure that the child knows she is 'camped out' in the minds of her important people – mentally being 'held' and thought about all day by those at home, as she lives her day at school. This knowledge is very important for very young children.

The 'key person' system

Letting go can be hard; but for parents it is a great deal more manageable in settings operating the key person system. Allocating a 'key person' to each child is essential for the youngest children from birth to three (Sure Start, 2002); but some version of this strategy is enormously helpful for children over three, too. Young children need to be with adults who are warm, positive, sensitive, responsive and consistent; they need to know that their key person will take time for them, will listen, explain things, be friends. In a key person system in a pre-school setting, one practitioner is allocated to each child and his or her family as their 'important person'. This system, properly managed, is not only about facilitating information exchange, co-ordination and smooth organisation, but also about close involvement with child and family in a reciprocal way. Elfer *et al.* (2003, p. 19) describe this as 'an emotional relationship, as well as an organisational strategy'.

For the child there are many advantages to this system. The increase in regular quality time involving sensitive talking and listening with a familiar adult, pays off in the child's heightened sense of security and well-being that comes from consistency of care and a strong sense of belonging. The family gains too, by having a consistent and reliable contact person within the setting who knows both the child and the family. This relationship between the key person and the child's family is based on reciprocal involvement, trust and confidence, and when it works well everyone benefits on all levels. For staff, there is increased job satisfaction, a clearer role, and the sense that 'you really matter' to your key children and their families. Clearly there are disadvantages too: the occasional absence (through illness or working pattern logistics) and eventual loss of the key person needs carefully managing; and for staff there may be issues of emotional involvement and increased responsibilities that also will need to be managed. It can be argued that this is both the most important and the most challenging stage of childcare and education – and sometimes not enough support is offered to staff in this most challenging role.

This is a thoroughly practical and highly satisfactory system for day-care and education settings where the staff–child ratio allows for regular one-to-one time together. It is more challenging for teachers with direct responsibility for many more children. But one of the main challenges for children starting school is the change in the quality of their relationship with the person they see as their 'important adult'. And it is a characteristic of the best teachers that children in their care feel that their teachers *do* take time for them, listen to them, explain things, and be friends.

Settings and schools helping 'new' children

In relation to school transitions, three core principles for educators are proposed by Aline-Wendy Dunlop (in Dunlop and Fabian, 2003, p. 84). Firstly she emphasises the importance of starting with the child, by which she means:

listen[ing] carefully to what people who already know the child can share with them, to work hard to build a relationship with the child and to create a learning environment which supports children's awareness of their own learning . . . Secondly the recognition that new learning experiences will be at their most effective if they are linked to what children already know, and to the mental frameworks they already have . . . thirdly in promoting a 'learning how to learn' approach, educators will be involved in supporting children to maintain the sense of identity as a learner that they have been developing.

These principles, where adopted, constitute a fundamental approach to the Foundation Stage curriculum. Settings and schools can also help incoming children in a variety of practical ways. Most offer introductory visits, with the child's parents or carer staying all the time. The more informal these are the better, taking place as much or as little as the child needs. Children in settings who will soon be starting 'Big School' often visit the new school in a group, together with a member of their pre-school staff. During these visits children can meet their new teacher or key person, as well as other children who are starting at the same time; and can begin to become familiar with the building and their own particular part of it. Very important questions for children are 'What does my new teacher look like?'; 'Where are the toilets?'; 'What happens at play-time?'; 'How will I know what to do next?' Well-managed visits of this sort help with knowing what to expect, underpinning the sense of confidence that helps every child on their first day.

Feeling welcomed and wanted on the first day is vital – and so often a simple tweaking of the system can do it. New children at the front of the line and new children choosing first, making sure that the new pegs or lockers are all ready and accessible – these things boost confidence and help to make a child feel special. Something that helps many children is a 'buddying' system, in which each child is given a 'buddy' – another child who is a confident 'old hand' for the first few weeks. This can work very well especially when the buddies themselves are well-supported, and is a great way of making sure that a new child feels looked after and special, particularly in the playground. Another way to welcome children is to make sure that *everyone* – adults and children – knows when new children are starting. Then everyone is ready to smile and say hello when they meet a new child. Usually new children are welcomed by the reception teacher herself but the rest of the school may not be particularly aware of them as people who need to be welcomed; but this simple difference is amazingly powerful and effective in helping to make children feel wanted and special.

Many children who are excited and optimistic about starting school do not quite grasp – until it happens – that starting school means leaving their pre-school setting. Leaving loved places and people is hard for all of us, and young children are no exception. Staff in pre-school settings can do much to help as children leave, by keeping goodbyes calm but genuine, making sure children know they will be missed and remembered but not getting upset themselves, and making sure children know that they will always be welcome to come back and see their old friends. (Most children never in fact do this, but it makes such a difference at the time to know that they can if they want to.) There is a lovely, traditional round that four- and five-year-olds love to sing, which sums up the situation nicely:

Make new friends, but keep the old
One is silver and the other gold

Home–school relationships

Children manage transitions much better if their parents feel confident about them, and here schools and settings can help families too. Making a relationship between home and school is of course important, and one significant element here is timing. Sometimes it makes sense to let relationships develop naturally over time, but this is not the case for parents and teachers as children start school. Making a positive start with getting to know each other as early as possible helps enormously, sharing as much as they can about each other and about the child's efforts and achievements, right from the start. Then, sooner or later if a problem arises, it can be dealt with in the context of an existing relationship between family and school. This is so much easier when parents and teachers have made a positive start and already know each other at least a little.

If parents are to do a good job supporting their children as they start school, they need a lot of information from the school – about what will happen and when, where to find things, what is expected, and so on. Most schools have some sort of welcoming occasion the previous term such as New Parents' Tea, and an information pack for new parents that contains this sort of information. In one school the most valued item in the 'Welcome to our School' pack was a little welcome booklet containing lively drawings and advice, put together by the children themselves. Here are some examples of advice:

Every morning we have to get to school before 8.55 a.m., the register is called at 8.55 a.m. We can come at twenty to nine if we want to.

If you need to go to the toilet, just ask the teacher. If you are in Mrs Hibbard's class, the boys' toilet is opposite your classroom door and the girls' toilet is next to the Guinea Pigs.

If you are put in the naughty behaviour book three times, your mum and dad have to come and talk to Mrs B.

Every so often you get to go in the music room where there is a load of musical instruments.

At the end of each day your teacher reads a story book to you.

The pictures are wonderful. And you can hear the child's voice, so much more reassuring than the usual formal notes to parents. Another good idea is to invite parents to come and eat lunch with their children sometimes in the early days. Also it helps children when the school has told parents who the adults at school are, and what they do. When a child is told 'Take this note to Mrs Brown, you know, the person in the office who smiles at us through the glass' it sounds so much more reassuring than 'Take this note to the office'; and 'Mrs Green will help you' carries more reassurance than 'Ask the teacher'.

Parents need to know how important it is that they do not discuss any concerns they have about their child within the child's hearing. This seems obvious and yet, when a parent is worried, it can be very difficult to be only positive within the child's hearing. Schools can help by mentioning this routinely at some stage in the induction process, so that it does not feel like a criticism, more a piece of information about something important – it could be part of the general information about how parents can contact teachers when they need to, if they would like to discuss something or if anything is worrying them; for instance: 'If you have a worry about your child or the school, please come and tell us about it – and please be careful not to let your child hear you worrying, as this makes children feel anxious'.

It seems that the most challenging aspects of school for new children are often the playground, lunch-times, and going to the toilet. Making sure these aspects go smoothly in the first weeks definitely pays off later, as early negative experiences of these parts of the school day can so easily undermine a child's ability to learn and to make the most of school life in the longer term, undoing in just a few minutes years of previous confidence-building. Every school has different systems, routines, expectations and rules, and yet every school could, in an ideal world, have at least one thing in common: the determination to make sure that all children – and especially new children – are supported so that play-times and lunch-times are enjoyable, and going to the toilet is not a problem. Although systems, routines, expectations and rules vary so much and some are helpful in terms of confidence-building and some are not, basically it hinges on relationships – on what people, both adults and children, say to each other and how they treat each other. There needs to be a whole-school awareness of new children and their families, so that they are consistently warmly welcomed, and made to feel that they belong. When children and their families are starting school, if this is right, for the most part all the rest will follow.

Much of the best work with parents and families in schools and settings owes a (frequently unconscious) debt of gratitude to the work of Chris Athey and also Tina Bruce in the Froebel 'Early Education Project' in the early 1970s (Athey, 1990). In a book from the Pen Green Centre team about working with parents, Margy Whalley (1997) offers advice to early childhood educators about actively involving parents in their settings, by:

- Home visiting
- Providing parent-friendly spaces within your setting
- Offering parents a range of groups that focus on their own learning needs and their children's learning needs

- Encouraging parents to run services for others and take on management roles in your setting

These four strategies all require commitment and resources, but the benefits of this proactive approach to parent involvement are considerable – and sometimes quite subtle. Whalley (1997, p. 177) says: 'You need to recognise the great untapped energy and ability of all parents using our settings. You need to have high expectations of their interest in and commitment to their children's learning. You need to develop mutual understanding and share experiences with parents'. The community ethos in such schools and settings makes an enormous difference for incoming children and their families, with its powerful message that 'this place is for us, we belong here'.

– LISA'S LECTURE –

❢ Lisa's in trouble with her college work. It turns out that as well as keeping a sort of diary about Lily and Joe, she has to think and read about why children want to learn. She's got some books, and she has to have her own ideas too – so it's about children she knows. She's worried because she has to give a sort of lecture about it to the other people at her college when she gets back next week, and she hasn't worked out what she's going to say. She showed me and Mum the books last night, and I said I'd help if she wants.

Then Mum said she thinks it's just what I'm interested in, and we'll all help Lisa to find good bits in the books that make us think about Lily and Joe, so she can make the most of knowing all about them. She says it won't be hard because the books aren't just about what children are supposed to know and do, they're about how children think and feel and how families and schools help as well.

Mum says how people do things around little children makes a really important difference to those children, and that wanting to learn is about **all** the things that are happening to children, and all the things that have happened before, right from the start. Like Mum says, I do think it's interesting, and I know a lot about that stuff. Maybe that's what I'll do next – go to college like Lisa. ❞

Wanting to learn makes all the difference to success

Learning dispositions of parents and carers

The following things help children to make a flying start at school: self-confidence and the disposition to learn; the ability to listen and talk and get on with other people; understanding about the uses of reading, writing, numbers and books; interest in the world. And returning briefly to Margaret Carr's terms discussed in Chapter

11, parents and carers who are *ready* to help children with these things will have been persuaded that they make a difference; parents and carers who are *willing* to help children with these things will know how to spot the right moment; and parents and carers who are *able* to help children with these things will know what is needed, how to help, and why. Such persuasion, skill and ability requires a high level of knowledge and understanding of child development; and it must be apparent that all parents and carers who live and work with the youngest children should be entitled to support in this most important area of work.

All parents want the best for their children. This is not in dispute, although what *is* sometimes disputed is the way this desire causes parents to act. Nonetheless, wanting the best for their child is a disposition that many thousands of parents have, and it represents an enormous, largely unrealised, source of energy for good. It could be released by offering relevant, appropriate and accessible information and support for parents and carers, when and where they need it.

One of the most important times to offer this information and support is when the child is just born. The birth of the baby is when the parent's disposition to do a good job in supporting a child's development is most likely to be full of optimism and joy and determination. Margaret Carr (2001) writes about dispositions as an accumulation of motivation, situation and skill in which the person with the disposition is 'ready, willing and able'. Carr's focus is on children's dispositions, but the same thinking can be used in relation to adults supporting a child's development. *Readiness* would mean being motivated or inclined to support the child; *willingness* would mean recognising when a time and situation are appropriate for support to be offered; and *ability* would mean having the knowledge, skills and understanding to support effectively. These three factors add up to possessing the disposition to support the child's development.

Babies' learning dispositions are strongly in place at birth; and adults can protect those dispositions and make the most of them, so that they retain their strength through the early years and into school. Margaret Carr talks of 'dispositional milieu' in which 'parents and carers provide opportunities for interest, involvement, persistence with difficulty, communication and responsibility' (2001, p. 36). In addition, parents and carers' *own* learning dispositions are of the greatest importance. Babies and young children living with adults who are ready, willing and able to explore, experiment, persist, learn from mistakes, question, watch and listen, are much more likely to retain these characteristics themselves.

Issues relating to learning dispositions come sharply into focus during times of transition, when children need to be 'ready, willing and able' (Carr 2001) to explore, experiment and learn from their mistakes. This is when children's important adults can help so much by exhibiting those same characteristics. In the PEEP model referred to earlier, 'modelling' is an important strand for supporting children's development. In times of uncertainty, this can be especially helpful for children. Their ability to tolerate and be motivated by uncertainty, 'caught' from adults modelling it, must surely be enormously advantageous in transition situations such as starting school.

Crucially, it is as children play that their learning dispositions are forming, and this is one reason why play is so essential to young children's learning. Perspectives on how very young children learn, and some of the ways in which adults can support that learning, are discussed in Part 4 (Linking with learning), in Chapters 7 and 8. What we mean by play, how it relates to self-esteem and learning, what children need for it and how adults can support it, are discussed in Part 5 (Real self-esteem), in Chapters 9 and 10.

Families matter

Nearly all children spend almost all of their time from birth to school at home. This is especially the case from birth to three years. During this time, babies and young children learn an astonishing amount, about themselves, the people around them, and the world in which they live. From total helplessness and in an amazingly short time, they learn to walk, to talk, and to take part in family life in increasingly sophisticated ways.

In spite of what we know about the rapid rate of brain development and of these solid early achievements, government-funded support for children's development, and the literature about early learning, appears to reflect a view that 'education' begins when a child makes contact with some sort of education provision outside the home. This does not of course make sense in terms of the real lives of children at home, from the day they are born. An enormous opportunity exists to lay solid foundations for later learning throughout life by acknowledging parents' crucial role from birth. Parents are the real specialists – in their own children. They are the people 'in the hot seat' when this crucial 'foundation' learning is taking place. Settings and programmes in the UK are beginning to acknowledge this and to develop ways of supporting parents, but there is a long way to go before even a modest level of support is offered universally.

Whether we like it or not, babies and young children do not wait to learn until we are ready to teach them. They get straight on with it from day one, learning from all the people, places and events around them from the very start. Nor are they selective, picking up only the things we would like them to absorb. They are like little sponges, soaking up everything indiscriminately. Joe may know a very wide range of stories and songs, but he also knows that if he makes a big fuss, he'll probably get something he wants, like playing his favourite game. He's getting very good at telling Mum at bed-time all about his day and what happened, but he was listening to Dan telling Lily about the playground yesterday and his account is likely to be sprinkled with the swear-words that are now part of Dan's and Lily's vocabulary. (Dan and Lily have also learned something else, which is that grown-ups don't like to hear children using those words even though they themselves do sometimes – but Joe is too young for this subtlety.)

The only way to make sure that *all* babies and young children are given the support that will help them to do well at school is to make sure that *all* parents have access to the information and ideas they need to enable them to provide that support. Currently only a proportion of parents access this information, and an important development of the work of children and family services will always be to find more ways of enabling access for all families, in ways that are appropriate to them. Young children love to have someone who listens, and lots of talk, stories, songs and rhymes, and playing together. These are some of the things that help children to make a flying start at school.

A vision for the twenty-first century

What is our vision for early childhood care and education in the twenty-first century? One of the most fundamental changes in recent decades in early childhood care and education has been the prominence now given to personal, social and emotional aspects of teaching and learning. With this new prominence comes a greater awareness both of outcomes in early childhood and of the need to focus on the *processes* of learning in order to reach those outcomes. Alongside this have been changes in perception in relation to the key players in early childhood: first, a more holistic view of the child, together with a greater understanding of the diversity of our society; second, a greater understanding of the primary importance of parents and the family in relation to babies and young children's development; and finally a realisation of the need for increasingly integrated services for children and families.

An enormous upsurge of thinking, discussion and writing in relation to early childhood is reflected in new documentation relating to holistic development from birth to school. This builds on a long tradition of good practice in early childhood care and education while at the same time incorporating new evidence about child development, and new perspectives on goals for education in the twenty-first century. Inevitably there will continue to be tensions and debates relating to the needs of young children and their families, and the most appropriate ways and times at which those needs can be met.

Support for children's development from birth to three is a comparatively recent focus, and is subject to added complexities. Firstly, most of the youngest children in our society spend most of their time at home with their parents, and so the challenge relates to the kinds of appropriate, effective and accessible support that can be offered to those families. Secondly, there are strong arguments for questioning the wisdom of policies that advocate day-care outside the home for many very young children, particularly for babies in their first year. As a strategy to combat child poverty by enabling mothers to return to work, the economic advantages are evident; and so is the value for children who desperately need alternative care. But in relation to the longer-term health and well-being of most children, the policy is deeply worrying.

There *is* a strong case to be made for a universal service to support children's development from birth to school. And indeed there is already in existence a universal service for the youngest children – that provided by their parents and carers at home. Babies and young children's development and learning is inextricably woven into the fabric of their everyday lives in the many rich and diverse parenting traditions of our multi-cultural society. Developing relevant and appropriate support for parents and carers in such very diverse cultures and circumstances is both a vitally important and an enormously sensitive task. Starting from the birth of the child – or better still, at the ante-natal stage – and encompassing the holistic range of children's emotional, social and cognitive development in addition to health, such support needs to focus first and foremost on home and family, at the same time ensuring the highest quality services in Children's Centres and day-care outside the home for those children who need it.

At the end of the twentieth century, Howard Gardner wrote of 'throwing out limiting old assumptions and respecting the flexibility, creativity, adventurousness, resourcefulness and generativity of the young mind.' (Gardner, 1993a). Now at the beginning of the twenty-first century, our understanding of children and their learning stands as never before in a place of tantalising opportunity. Now we need holistic schools and services, for the whole child. From Plato to the present day early childhood development, arguably the most important of human preoccupations, has never before been perceived as so vital. Never before has it been thought so promising a field of study, so appropriate a subject for investment and research, so important an area of employment, so fundamental for the present and for the future of our society. And never before has the challenge to early childhood and family services been so great.

For many children, their first experiences of the wider world beyond their family of pre-school and school will be the beginning of their understanding of the rich diversity of our society. Before school, all children become deeply interested in the fascinating concepts of 'same' and 'different' in the world as they know it, whether it applies to biscuits, bibs, images, sounds, or indeed people. This is the basis of later increasingly complex categorisations. Children's experiences of people from cultures different from their own will vary enormously before they start school, and in terms of 'same' and 'different' the people at home will constitute the norm, for the time being. For the essentially egocentric child, it is a question of 'same as me?' or 'different from me?'. However, for young children this question carries none of the value-laden overtones of race or class that might be the case for an adult; they are simply finding out about their world. And as they enter school, the world that is theirs expands dramatically.

As long ago as 1979, Brian Jackson was writing an extraordinarily powerful account of six children starting school in a north of England town. The six children all came from very different communities, and they all lived in the same street – but on their first day at school they were new to one another. Jackson met them a few months before their first day at school, and stayed with them and their families throughout the first term. His book holds up a fascinating mirror to this richly diverse group of children; and since then in primary classrooms the rich diversity has only got better. These days it is entirely normal to meet children in every classroom for whom English is their second language (or indeed their third, if you count body language as the first and most important). These children are amazingly skilled linguistically; and if they are not quite fluent yet in English, they become so with astonishing speed.

A wonderful aspect of early childhood education and care is the opportunities it offers children to get to know other people (both children and adults) who are in some ways different and in some ways the same. This *social* aspect of starting school is hugely important, as powerful in its impact as aspects relating to early learning – indeed to a large extent it *is* early learning. At first, children and adults will be seen by a young child in terms of difference; but immediately this two-dimensional perception will begin to expand to include all the shared experiences of play and learning that go to make up the rich fabric of friendships. No longer are other children described in terms of difference as for instance 'that one with the funny hair' or 'that one with the bad leg' or 'that one who talks different'. Descriptions quickly move to reflect not exactly 'sameness' but important shared experiences, such as 'that one I played with' or 'that one who helped me' or 'that one who gave me his chocolate cake'. And soon after, these labels are no longer needed because real names take their place; and responsive parents can contact each other to offer shared experiences at home too, that can help to strengthen these new friendships.

Many children's and their families' shared experiences with the people they meet when they start school help to make a valuable contribution to the bedrock of present and future community harmony. But in the twenty-first century schools may need to guard against losing much of this dimension of 'friendship time' through the pressures of the curriculum. 'Friendship time' for children and their families needs deliberately and creatively to be nurtured as a precious aspect of school, and a vitally important element for the future of our society.

Meanwhile the pace of change around us is accelerating. Traditional authorities are undermined in a variety of ways: by demographic changes, by social and family modifications, by the global market place, by new technology, by challenges to security. All these factors are having a profound effect on our lives. Sometimes we seem to have lost our way in terms of values and family life. The need to find a new sense of direction highlights the urgency of many of the issues raised in this book.

In an article entitled 'Tilting the Balance', Tom Leimdorfer (1993) suggested ways of working towards a more hopeful vision of the future. He proposed five basic ingredients as priorities in our educational climate: an affirming climate (positive self-images, valuing ourselves and others), a listening climate, a co-operative climate, a problem-solving climate and a human rights climate. Over a decade later these continue to be a vision for the future, the essence of which has been foreshadowed many times in the past. Joan Riviere (1927, reprinted 1955) was the analyst of both Winnicott and Bowlby. Echoing John Donne, she wrote:

> *There is no such thing as a single human being, pure and simple, unmixed with other human beings. Each personality is a world in himself, a company of many. That self . . . is a composite structure . . . formed out of countless never-ending influences and*

exchanges between ourselves and others. These other persons are in fact therefore part of ourselves . . . we are members of one another. (Riviere, 1955)

These 'countless never-ending influences and exchanges between ourselves and others' begin at the moment of our birth and gather momentum throughout early childhood. They have been the subject of this book on early childhood, '. . . a period of momentous significance for all people growing up in [our] culture – by the time this period is over, children will have formed conceptions of themselves as social beings, as thinkers, and as language users, and they will have reached certain important decisions about their own abilities and their own worth' (Donaldson *et al.*, 1983, p. 1).

The importance of 'multi-mindedness' has been proposed: of thinking about others around us at the same time as ourselves; of meeting every child's need for acceptance and attachment while making the case for adults' careful observation of children, and for setting limits. Children who have learned from their important adults to value their own and others' genuine efforts and achievements are more likely to believe in themselves as learners, and to learn successfully . . . not only as they start school, but throughout school and for the rest of their lives.

Epilogue

6 Tomorrow I'm going away to college. They gave me some money to get things, and I've done the washing and got my stuff together, so I'm ready. Lisa says she'll help me settle in.

I'm going to miss everyone, especially Lily and Joe. Lily says she's coming with me. She hasn't figured out that you can't be in two places at once, so if she comes with me she won't have Mum and her dad; she thinks she can be with me and be at home as well.

She's right, though, as usual. She's coming with me in my head. I'll never forget them – Mum and Dad and Lily and Joe. 9

POSTSCRIPT TO PART 6: NEW JOURNEYS

Living or working with young children?
Questions to think about . . .

> Children in transition need to know what to expect,
> with *time* and *support* to reflect on their experiences
> and to look forward to new ones; and *confidence* that
> adults will understand and respect their needs

1. When a child's world is about to change, what can adults do to help? Try applying this question to particular situations, for instance a new baby in the family, moving home, starting school.

> Talking, listening, playing and singing together, and
> sharing books every day . . . from birth all children
> need opportunities to do these things, with people
> they love and admire who recognise, value and
> encourage their efforts and achievements

2. What do babies and young children really mind about?

> *Wanting* to learn makes all the difference to success

3. Why is it that some children seem to want to learn and some don't? What is the basis of a life-long disposition to learn?

RECOMMENDED FURTHER READING

For sharing with children . . .

Briggs, R. (1970), *Jim and the Beanstalk***, London, Puffin Books**
Jim has all the positive learning dispositions – he's exploratory, questioning, a listener, and a persistent problem solver Undoubtedly ready, willing and able to help the giant, Jim does, however, lack an element of foresight, and only just escapes being fried and served up on toast for breakfast. But he very properly ends up with his just reward, to his mother's relief. Children love the suspense, and it's full of humour for adults too.

Sendak, M. (1963), *Where the Wild Things Are***, London, Red Fox**
'The night Max wore his wolf suit and made mischief . . .' begins Max's epic journey. This classic book has been read and re-read and loved to tatters over half a century, and not just by children. The excitement of the journey, the ferocity of the wild things who were tamed 'with the magic trick of staring into all their yellow eyes without blinking once', the wild rumpus, and the return to where someone loved him best of all – these things surely appeal to all of us.

. . . and for a good read

Carr, M. (2001), *Assessment in Early Childhood Settings: Learning Stories***, London, Paul Chapman Publishing**
Abandoning the general notion of a body of requisite knowledge and skills for school entry, Margaret Carr suggests that the ultimate goals of early education should have much more to do with learning dispositions such as resilience, confidence and collaboration. Her important book is a timely reminder of the complexities and ambitions of young children and their learning, and the skilful and sensitive role of adults in effectively supporting and assessing them.

Key statements

PART 1   BABIES FIRST

Babies and young children need to feel accepted
by their important people

How babies and young children learn to see themselves
is significantly affected by their
growing knowledge of how to be acceptable
to us

Babies and young children generally behave according
to how they see themselves

PART 2　FUNDAMENTAL FEELINGS

As well as feeling love, it is normal for people to feel pain, anxiety and anger

Denied pain, anxiety and anger all undermine positive self-concept – these feelings are hard to acknowledge and manage unless they are recognised by others as normal and acceptable

Babies and young children can manage pain, anxiety and anger more easily if they know that other people accept and sympathise with how they feel

PART 3　ABOUT OTHER PEOPLE

'Unreasonable' behaviour is almost always reasonable from the point of view of the baby or young child doing it

It is possible to accept and sympathise with babies' and young children's pain, anxiety and anger without having to accept 'unreasonable' behaviour generated by those feelings

Children learn to be responsible by taking responsibility

PART 4   LINKING WITH LEARNING

Learning involves struggle and adjustment. Too much struggle is overwhelming. Too little struggle means no adjustment

Some learning skills come naturally; these include exploring, questioning, experimenting and learning from mistakes

In order to be 'socially acceptable', children often learn to behave in ways that inhibit learning

PART 5   REAL SELF-ESTEEM

Children are encouraged to learn when someone knows what they especially want to do and can nearly manage, and helps them to manage it successfully

Recognising and supporting the development of children's patterns of learning, or schemas, leads to high self-esteem

Children learn well with a combination of appropriately high expectations and appropriately high self-esteem

PART 6   NEW JOURNEYS

Children in transition need to know what to expect, with *time* and *support* to reflect on their experiences and to look forward to new ones; and *confidence* that adults will understand and respect their needs

Talking, listening, playing and singing together, and sharing books every day . . . from birth all children need opportunities to do these things, with people they love and admire who recognise, value and encourage their efforts and achievements

Wanting to learn makes all the difference

Bibliography and references

Abbott, L. and Pugh, C. (1998), *Training to Work in the Early Years*, Buckingham, Open University Press

Abbott, L. and Moylett, H. (1999), *Early Education Transformed*, London, Falmer Press

Abbott, L. and Nutbrown, C. (2001), *Experiencing Reggio Emilia*, Buckingham, Open University Press

Ahlberg, J. and A. (1978), *Each Peach Pear Plum*, London, Puffin Books

Athey, C. (1990), *Extending Thought in Young Children*, London, Paul Chapman Publishing, 2nd edn in press

BBC/National Children's Bureau (1999), *Tuning into Children*, London, BBC Education Production

Bagley, C., Verma, G., Mallick, M. and Young, L. (1979), *Personality, Self-esteem and Prejudice*, London, Saxon House

Ball, C. (1994), *Start Right: The Importance of Early Learning*, London, RSA

Bannister, D. and Fransella, F. (1986), *Inquiring Man: The Psychology of Personal Constructs*, London, Croom Helm

Barnes, P. (1995), *Personal, Social and Emotional Development of Children*, Oxford, Basil Blackwell

Bartholomew, L. and Bruce, T. (1993), *Getting to Know You*, London, Hodder and Stoughton

Becker, E. (1971), *The Birth and Death of Meaning*, London, Penguin Books

Bettelheim, B. (1987), *A Good Enough Parent*, London, Thames and Hudson

Bick, E. (1963), 'Notes on Infant Observation in Psychoanalytic Training' in M. Harris Williams (ed.), *Collected Papers of Martha Harris and Esther Bick*, Strath Tay, The Clunie Press

Bion, W.R. (1962), *Learning From Experience*, London, Heinemann

Bird, J. and Gerlach, L. (2005), *Improving the Emotional Health and Wellbeing of Young People in Secure Care: Training for staff in local authority secure children's homes*, London, National Children's Bureau

Black, D. (1991), 'The Red Judge' in *Collected Poems: 1964–87*, Edinburgh, Polygon

Blakemore, S.-J. (2000), *Early Years Learning*, London, Parliamentary Office of Science and Technology

Blakemore, S.-J. and Frith, U. (2005), *The Learning Brain: Lessons for Education*, Oxford, Blackwell Publishing

Blau, D. (2001), *The Child Care Problem*, New York, Russell Sage Foundation Press

Blenkin, G. and Kelly, A.V. (1992), *Assessment in Early Childhood Education*, London, Paul Chapman Publishing

Bower, T. (1977), *A Primer of Infant Development*, San Francisco, CA, Freeman

Bowlby, J. (1969), *Attachment*, London, Penguin Books

Bowlby, J. (1973), *Separation*, London, Penguin Books

Bowlby, J. (1980), *Loss*, London, Penguin Books

Brazelton, T. (1992), *Touchpoints*, London, Viking

Brice Heath, S. (1983), *Ways With Words*, Cambridge, Cambridge University Press

Briggs, R. (1970), *Jim and the Beanstalk*, London, Puffin Books

Briggs, R. (1978), *The Snowman*, London, Hamish Hamilton

Brooks, G., Gorman, T., Harman, J., Hutchinson, D. and Wilkin, A. (1996), *Family Literacy Works*, London, The Basic Skills Agency

Brown, B. (1998), *Unlearning Discrimination in the Early Years*, Stoke on Trent, Trentham Books Ltd

Browne, E. (1994), *Handa's Surprise*, London, Walker Books

Bruce, T. (1987), *Early Childhood Education*, London, Hodder and Stoughton

Bruce, T. (1991), *Time To Play in Early Childhood Education*, London, Hodder and Stoughton

Bruce, T. (1996), *Helping Young Children to Play*, London, Hodder and Stoughton

Bruce, T. (2001), *Learning Through Play – Babies, Toddlers, and the Foundation Years*, London, Hodder and Stoughton

Bruce, T. (2004), *Developing Learning in Early Childhood*, London, Paul Chapman Publishing

Bruce, T. and Meggitt, C. (1999), *Child Care and Education* (Second Edition), London, Hodder and Stoughton

Bruner, J. (1962), *On Knowing*, Cambridge, MA, Belknap Press

Bruner, J. (1971), *The Relevance of Education*, London, Allen and Unwin

Bruner, J. and Haste, H. (1987), *Making Sense*, London, Routledge

Buchanan, A. and Hudson, B.L. (1998), *Parenting, Schooling and Children's Behaviour*, Aldershot, Ashgate Publishing Ltd

Burningham, J. (1973), *Mr Gumpy's Outing*, London, Puffin Books

Campbell, R. (1982), *Dear Zoo*, London, Macmillan Children's Books

Canfield, J. and Wells, H. (1976), *100 Ways to Enhance Self-Concept in the Classroom*, Englewood Cliffs, NJ, Prentice Hall

Carr, M. (2001), *Assessment in Early Childhood Settings: Learning Stories*, London, Paul Chapman Publishing

Chukovsky, K. (1966), *From Two to Five*, Berkeley, CA, University of California Press

Claxton, G. (1984), *Live and Learn*, London, Harper and Row

Claxton, G. (1997), *Hare Brain, Tortoise Mind – Why Intelligence Increases when you Think Less*, London, Fourth Estate

Crocker, A.C. and Cheeseman, R.G. (1988), 'Infant teachers have a major impact on children's self-awareness' in *Children & Society*, 2, 3–8

Curry, N. and Johnson, C. (1990), *Beyond Self-Esteem: Developing a Genuine Sense of Human Value*, Washington, DC, NAEYC

Curtis, A. (1992), 'How Competent Are Our Young Children?' in *Early Education*, 5, 9–10

David, T. (1990), *Under Five – Under-educated?*, Buckingham, Open University Press

David, T., Raban, B., Ure, C., Goouch, K., Jago, M. and Barriere, I. (2000), *Making Sense of Early Literacy*, Stoke on Trent, Trentham Books Ltd

Desforges, C. (1989), 'Understanding Learning for Teaching' in *Westminster Studies in Education*, 12, 2, 17–29

DES (1989), *The Education of Children Under Five*, London, HMSO

DES.(1990), *Starting With Quality: The Report of Enquiry into the Quality of the Educational Experience Offered to Three- and Four-Year-Olds*, London, HMSO

Docking, J. (1980), *Control and Discipline*, London, Harper and Row

Donaldson, M. (1978), *Children's Minds*, London, Fontana Press

Donaldson, M., Grieve, R. and Pratt, C. (1983), *Early Childhood Development and Education: Readings in Psychology*, Oxford, Basil Blackwell

Donaldson, M. and Elliot, T. (1990), 'Children's Explanations' in R. Grieve and M. Hugh (eds), *Understanding Children*, Oxford, Blackwell

Dowling, M. (2005), *Young Children's Personal, Social and Emotional Development* (Second Edition), London, Paul Chapman Publishing

Driver, R. (1983), *The Pupil as Scientist*, Oxford, Oxford University Press

Drummond, M.J. (1993), *Assessing Children's Learning*, London, David Fulton Publishers

Drummond, M.J. (1999), *Comparisons in Early Years Education: History, Fact and Fiction*, University of Warwick, Centre for Research in Elementary and Primary Education

Dunlop, A-W. and Fabian, H. (eds) (2002), *Transitions in the Early Years*, London, RoutledgeFalmer

Dunlop, A-W. and Fabian, H. (eds) (2003), *Transitions. European Early Childhood Education Journal, Themed Monograph Series*, 1.

Dunn, J. (1984), *Sisters and Brothers*, London, Fontana

Dunn, J. (1988), *The Beginnings of Social Understanding*, Oxford, Blackwell

Dunn, J. (1993), *Young Children's Close Relationships*, London, Sage Publications

Dunn, J. (2004), *Children's Friendships: The Beginnings of Intimacy*, Oxford, Blackwell Publishing

Early Childhood Education Forum (1998), *Quality in Diversity in Early Learning*, London, National Children's Bureau

Edelman, G. (1992), *Bright Air, Brilliant Fire: On the Matter of the Mind*, London, The Penguin Press

Edwards, A.G. (2002), *Relationships and Learning: Caring for Children from Birth to Three*, London, National Children's Bureau

Elfer, P., Goldschmied, E. and Selleck, D. (2003), *Key Persons in the Nursery: Building Relationships for Quality Provision*, London, David Fulton Publishers

English, H.B. and A.C. (1958), *A Comprehensive Dictionary of Psychological and Psychoanalytical Terms*, London, Longman

Erikson, E. (1950), *Childhood and Society*, London, Paladin

Feinstein, L. (2000), *The Relative Importance of Academic, Psychological and Behavioural Attributes Developed in Childhood*, London, Centre for Economic Performance

Fisher, J. (1996), *Starting from the Child*, Buckingham, Open University Press

Fisher, J. (ed.), (2002), *The Foundations of Learning*, Buckingham, Open University Press

Fountain, S. (1990), *Learning Together*, Cheltenham, Stanley Thornes

Freud, S. (1977), *Case Histories* 1, London, Penguin Books

Galloway, F. (1987), 'PSE Teaching Pack' in Appendix 3 *Personal and Social Education in the Primary School*, University of York, Diploma in Applied Educational Studies

Gardner, H. (1993a), *Frames of Mind: The Theory of Multiple Intelligence*, New York, Basic Books

Gardner, H. (1993b), 'Complementary Perspectives on Reggio Emilia' in C. Edwards, L. Gandini and G. Forman (eds), *The Hundred Languages of Children – The Reggio Emilia Approach to Early Childhood Education*, New Jersey, Ablex

Gerhardt, S. (2004), *Why Love Matters: How Affection Shapes a Baby's Brain*, London, Routledge

Goldschmied, E. and Jackson, S. (2004), *People Under Three: Young Children in Day Care* (Second Edition), London, Routledge

Gopnik, A., Meltzoff, A. and Kuhl, P. (1999), *How Babies Think*, London, Weidenfeld and Nicolson

Gore, A. (1992), *Earth in the Balance*, London, Earthscan

Grieve, R. and Hughes, M. (1990), *Understanding Children*, Oxford, Blackwell

Gura, P. (ed.) (1992), *Exploring Learning: Young Children and Blockplay*, London, Paul Chapman Publishing

Hannon, P. (1995), *Literacy, Home and School*, London, Falmer Press

Harris, M. (1987), 'Some Notes on Maternal Containment' in M. Harris Williams (ed.), *Collected Papers of Martha Harris and Esther Bick*, Strath Tay, The Clunie Press

Harris, P.L. (1989), *Children and Emotion – The Development of Psychological Understanding*, Oxford, Basil Blackwell

Herbert, M. (1996a), *Feuding and Fighting: A Guide to the Management of Aggression and Quarrelling in Children*, London, The British Psychological Society

Herbert, M. (1996b) *Setting Limits: Promoting Positive Parenting*, London, The British Psychological Society

Hitz, R. and Driscoll, A. (1988), 'New Insights Into Praise: Implications for Early Childhood Teachers' in *Young Children*, July

Holditch, L. (1992), *Understanding Your Five-Year-Old*, London, Rosendale Press

Holmes, J. (1993), *John Bowlby and Attachment Theory*, London, Routledge

Holt, J. (1983), *How Children Learn*, London, Penguin Books

Honess, T. and Yardley, K. (1987), *Self and Identity: Perspectives across the Lifespan*, London, Routledge and Kegan Paul

House of Commons Education and Employment Committee (2000), *First Report: Early Years*, London, The Stationery Office

Hudson, L. (1975), *Human Beings*, London, Jonathan Cape

Hughes, S. (1993), *Giving*, London, Walker Books

Hurst, V. (1991), *Planning for Early Learning*, London, Paul Chapman Publishing

Isaacs, S. (1954), *The Educational Value of the Nursery School*, London, The British Association for Early Childhood Education

Jackson, B. (1979), *Starting School*, London, Croom Helm

Jowett, S. and Sylva, K. (1986), 'Does Kind of Pre-School Matter?' in *Educational Research*, 28, 1, 21–31

Karoly, L.A., Greenwood, P.W., Everingham, S.S, Hoube, J., Kiburn, M.R., Rydell, C.P., Sanders, M. and Chiesa, J. (1998), *Investing in our Children: What we Know and Don't Know about the Costs and Benefits of Early Childhood Interventions*, Washington, DC, RAND

Katz, L.G. (1993), *Dispositions as Educational Goals*, Urbana, IL, ERIC Digest

Katz, L.G. (1995), *Talks with Teachers of Young Children*, Norwood, NJ, Ablex Publishing Corporation

Kelly, G.A. (1955), *The Psychology of Personal Constructs*, New York, Norton

Kelly, G.A. (1970), 'A brief introduction to personal construct theory' in D. Bannister (ed.), *Perspectives in Personal Construct Theory*, London, Academic Press

Klein, M. (1975a), *Love, Guilt and Reparation*, London, Virago

Klein, M. (1975b), *Envy and Gratitude*, London, Virago

Konner, M. (1991), *Childhood*, London, Little, Brown and Company

Laevers, F. (2000), 'Forward to Basics! Deep-Level Learning and the Experiential Approach', in *Early Years* 20, 2, 20–9

Lally, M. (1991), *The Nursery Teacher in Action*, London, Paul Chapman Publishing

Lawrence, D. (1987), *Enhancing Self-Esteem in the Classroom*, London, Paul Chapman Publishing

Leach, P. (2003), *Your Baby and Child*, London, Dorling Kindersley

Lee, V. and Das Gupta, P. (1995), *Children's Cognitive and Language Development*, Buckingham, Open University Press

Leimdorfer, T. (1993), 'Tilting the Balance' in *The Friend*, 27 August

Leslie, A. (1987), 'Pretence and Representation: The Origins of "Theory of Mind"' in *Psychological Review*, 94, 4, 412–26

Lewis-Stempel, J. (2004), *Fatherhood: An Anthology*, New York, Overlook Press

Light, P. (1979), *The Development of Social Sensitivity*, Cambridge, Cambridge University Press

Lindon, J. (2000), *Helping Babies and Toddlers Learn*, London, National Early Years Network

Logan, R. (1987), 'Historical Change in Prevailing Sense of Self' in K. Yardley and T. Honess (eds), *Self and Identity: Psychological Perspectives*, Chichester, John Wiley

MacFarlane, J.A. (1977), *The Psychology of Childbirth*, Oxford, Oxford University Press

Magee, B. (1973), *Popper*, London, Fontana

Makins, V. (1997), *Not Just a Nursery Rhyme*, London, National Children's Bureau

Malaguzzi, L. (1987), *The Hundred Languages of Children: Narrative of the Possible*, Catalogue of the 'Hundred Languages of Children' exhibition, Reggio Emilia, Comune di Reggio Emilia

Markus, H. and Nurius, P. (1987), 'Possible Selves: The Interface between Motivation and the Self-concept' in K. Yardley and T. Honess (eds), *Self and Identity*, Chichester, John Wiley

Marshall, H. (1989), 'The Development of Self-Concept' in *Young Children*, July

Maslow, A. (1968), *Toward a Psychology of Being*, New York, Van Nostrand Reinhold

Matthews, J. (1987), 'The Young Child's Early Representation and Drawing' in G. Blenkin and A.V. Kelly (eds), *Early Childhood Education: A Development Curriculum*, London, Paul Chapman Publishing

Matthews, J. (1994), *Helping Children to Draw and Paint: Visual Representation*, London, Hodder and Stoughton

Mead, G. (1934), *Mind, Self and Society*, Chicago, IL, University of Chicago Press

Meade, A. (2000), *The Brain Debate*, Wellington, Fulbright Lecture

Medawar, P. (1981), *Pluto's Republic*, Oxford, Oxford University Press

Miedzian, M. (1992), *Boys Will Be Boys*, London, Virago

Miller, A. (1979), *The Drama of Being a Child*, London, Virago

Miller, L. (1992a), *Understanding Your Baby*, London, Rosendale Press

Miller, L. (1992b), *Understanding Your Four-Year-Old*, London, Rosendale Press

Moyles, J. (ed.) (1994), *The Excellence of Play*, Buckingham, Open University Press

Nash, R. (1976), *Teacher Expectations and Pupil Learning*, London, Routledge and Kegan Paul

National Commission on Education (1993), *Learning to Succeed*, London, Heinemann

New Zealand Ministry of Education (1996), *Te Whariki: Early Childhood Curriculum*, Wellington, Learning Media

Noddings, N. (2003), *Happiness and Education*, Cambridge, Cambridge University Press

Nutbrown, C. (1994), *Threads of Thinking*, London, Paul Chapman Publishing

Ormerod, J. (1997), *Peek-a-boo*, London, The Bodley Head

Paley, V.G. (1992), *You Can't Say You Can't Play*, Cambridge, MA, Harvard University Press

Paley, V.G. (2004), *A Child's Work: The Importance of Fantasy Play*, Chicago, IL, Chicago University Press

Pascal, C. (1990), *Under-Fives in the Infant Classroom*, Stoke on Trent, Trentham Books Ltd

Pascal, C. and Bertram, T. (1997), *Effective Early Learning: Case Studies in Improvement*, London, Hodder and Stoughton

Penn, H. (1997), *Comparing Nurseries: Staff and Children in Italy, Spain and the UK*, London, Paul Chapman Publishing

Perez-Sanchez, M. (1990), *Baby Observation: Emotional Relationships During the First Year of Life*, Strath Tay, Clunie Press

Piaget, J. (1951), *Play, Dreams and Imitation in Childhood*, London, Routledge and Kegan Paul

Piaget, J. (1953), *The Origin of Intelligence in the Child*, London, Routledge and Kegan Paul

Pines, M. (1987), 'Mirroring and Child Development' in T. Honess and K. Yardley (eds), *Self and Identity*, London, Routledge and Kegan Paul

Pollard, A. and Tann, S. (1987), *Reflective Teaching in the Primary School*, London, Cassell Education

Purves, L. and Selleck, D. (1999), *Tuning in to Children: Understanding a Child's Development from Birth to Five*, London, BBC Education

QCA/DfES (2000), *Curriculum Guidance for the Foundation Stage*, London, Qualifications and Curriculum Authority

Rathmann, P. (1994) *Good Night, Gorilla*, London, Puffin Books

Reid, S. (1992), *Understanding Your Two-Year-Old*, London, Rosendale Press

Riviere, J. (1955), 'The unconscious phantasy of an inner world reflected in examples from literature' in M. Klein, P. Heimann and R. Money-Kyrle (eds), *New Directions in Psychoanalysis*, London, Hogarth

Roberts, R. (1993), 'Self-Concept and Learning Skills at Four Years Old', unpublished MA dissertation, Oxford Brookes University

Roberts, R. (ed.) (1995), *A Nursery Education Curriculum for the Early Years*, Oxford, National Primary Centre

Roberts, R. (ed.) (2000a), *The Learning Together Series*, Oxford, PEEP

Roberts, R. (ed.) (2000b), *PEEP Voices – A Five-Year Diary*, Oxford, PEEP

Roberts, R. (ed.) (2001), *Making the Most of PEEP*, Oxford, PEEP

Rogers, C. (1961), *On Becoming a Person*, London, Constable

Rycroft, C. (1968), *A Critical Dictionary of Psychoanalysis*, London, Penguin Books

Salmon, W. (1988), *Psychology for Teachers*, London, Hutchinson

Sammons, P. et al. (1999), *Technical Paper 2: Characteristics of the EPPE Project Sample at Entry to the Study*, London, Institute of Education, University of London

Scott, J. and Ward, H. (2005), *Safeguarding and Promoting the Wellbeing of Vulnerable Children*, London, Jessica Kingsley Publishers

Sendak, M. (1963), *Where the Wild Things Are*, London, Red Fox

Sheridan, M. (1991), 'Increasing Self-Esteem and Competency in Children' in *International Journal of Early Childhood*, 23, 1, 28–35

Shonkoff, J. and Phillips, D. (2000), *From Neurons to Neighbourhoods: The Science of Early Childhood Development*, Washington, DC, National Academy Press

Shore, R. (1997), *Rethinking the Brain – New Insights into Early Development*, New York, Families and Work Institute

Singer, D. and J. (1990), *The House of Make-Believe*, Cambridge, MA, Harvard University Press

Siraj-Blatchford, I. (ed.) (1998), *A Curriculum Development Handbook for Early Childhood Educators*, Stoke on Trent, Trentham Books Ltd

Siraj-Blatchford, I. and J. (1995), *Educating the Whole Child: Cross-Curricular Skills, Themes and Dimensions*, Buckingham, Open University Press

Siraj-Blatchford, I. and Clarke, P. (2000), *Supporting Identity, Diversity and Language in the Early Years*, Buckingham, Open University Press

Skemp, R. (1979), *Intelligence, Learning and Action*, Chichester, John Wiley

Smith, F. (1978), *Reading*, Cambridge, Cambridge University Press

Smolensky, E.E. and Gootman, J.E. (2003), *Working Families and Growing Kids: Caring for Children and Adolescents*, Washington, DC, National Academy Press

Steiner, D. (1992), *Understanding Your One-Year-Old*, London, Rosendale Press

Storr, A. (1960), *The Integrity of the Personality*, London, Penguin Books

Stott, D., Green, L. and Francis, J. (1988), *The Guide to the Child's Learning Skills*, Stafford, NARE Publications

Sure Start (2000a), *Providing Good Quality Childcare and Early Learning Experience through Sure Start*, Nottingham, DfEE Publications

Sure Start (2000b), *Sure Start – Making a Difference for Children and Families*, Nottingham, DfEE Publications

Sure Start (2002) *Birth to Three Matters: A Framework to Support Children in their Earliest Years*, London, Sure Start Unit

Sylva, K. (1994), 'The Impact of Early Learning on Children's Later Development' in C. Ball (ed.), *Start Right: The Importance of Early Learning*, London, RSA

Tizard, B. and Hughes, M. (1984), *Young Children Learning*, London, Fontana

Trevarthen, C. and Aitken, K. (2001), 'Infant Intersubjectivity: Research, Theory, and Clinical Applications' in *Journal of Child Psychology and Psychiatry*, 42, 1, 3–48

Trowell, J. (1992), *Understanding Your Three-Year-Old*, London, Rosendale Press

Vandell, D. and Wolfe, B. (2000), *Child Care Quality: Does It Matter and Does It Need to Be Improved?* Washington, DC, US Department of Health and Human Services

Vygotsky, L. (1978), *Mind in Society*, Cambridge, MA, Harvard University Press

Waddell, M. and Benson, P. (1992), *Owl Babies*, London, Walker Books

Waddell, M. and Firth, B. (1999), *Well Done, Little Bear*, London, Walker Books

Waldfogel, J. (2004) *Social Mobility, Life Chances, and the Early Years*, CASEpaper 88

Weinberger, J. (1996), *Literacy Goes to School: The Parents' Role in Young Children's Literacy Learning*, London, Paul Chapman Publishing

Waldegrave, W. (1991), *The Health of the Nation*, London, HMSO

Wells, G. (1986), *The Meaning Makers*, London, Hodder and Stoughton

Whalley, M. (1994), *Learning To Be Strong*, London, Hodder and Stoughton

Whalley, M. (1997), *Working with Parents*, London, Hodder and Stoughton

Whalley, M. (2000), *Involving Parents in their Children's Learning*, London, Paul Chapman Publishing

Winkley, L. (1991), 'Children's Emotional Needs: A Child Psychiatrist's View' *in Special Issue in Primary Education*, 1, 8–11

Winnicott, D.W. (1964), *The Child, the Family and the Outside World*, London, Penguin Books

Winnicott, D.W. (1971), 'Mirror-role of mother and family in child development' in *Playing and Reality*, London, Tavistock Publications

Winnicott, D.W. (1986), *Home Is Where We Start From*, London, Penguin Books

Wishinsky, F. and Thompson, C. (1998), *Oonga Boonga: Big Brother's Magic Words*, London, Picture Corgi

Wolfendale, S. and Bryans, T. (1989), *Managing Behaviour*, Stafford, NARE Publications

Wolff, R.P. (ed.) (1968), *Kant: A Collection of Critical Essays*, London, Macmillan

Wylie, C. (1996), *Five Years Old and Competent*, Wellington, New Zealand Council for Educational Research

Wylie, C. (1998), *Six Years Old and Competent*, Wellington, New Zealand Council for Educational Research

Yardley, K. and Honess, T. (1987), *Self and Identity: Psychological Perspectives*, Chichester, John Wiley

Ziman, E. (1950), *Jealousy in Children*, London, Gollancz

Index